CW01664381

PRICEWATERHOUSECOOPERS

UK interim financial statements 2010: illustrative accounts and checklist

UK Accounting Consulting Services
PricewaterhouseCoopers LLP, Chartered Accountants

CCH
a Wolters Kluwer business

145 London Road
Kingston-upon-Thames
Surrey
KT2 6SR
Tel: +44 (0) 870 777 2906
Fax: +44 (0) 870 247 1184
E-mail: info@cch.co.uk
Web site: www.cch.co.uk

ISBN 978-1-84798-324-4

Printed in Great Britain.

British Library Cataloguing-in-Publication Data.
A catalogue record for this book is available from the British Library.

Contents

	Page
Introduction	1
Illustrative interim financial information for the half-year ended 30 June 2010	7
Commentary – Notes to the consolidated financial statements	8
Interim management report	11
Consolidated income statement	15
Consolidated statement of comprehensive income	16
Consolidated balance sheet	17
Consolidated statement of changes in equity	18
Consolidated statement of cash flows	19
Notes to the consolidated interim financial statements	20
1 General information	20
2 Basis of preparation of half-year report	20
3 Accounting policies	20
4 Segment information	22
5 Profit for the half-year	24
6 Property, plant and equipment	25
7 Current provisions	25
8 Non-current borrowings	25
9 Equity securities issued	26
10 Dividends	26
11 Discontinued operations	27
12 Business combinations	28
13 Contingencies	30
14 Related-party transactions	30
15 Events occurring after the reporting period	30
Statement of directors' responsibility	31
Auditors' review report – ISRE (UK&I) 2410	32
Appendix I – Alternative presentation of consolidated income statement – expenses by nature	34
Appendix II – Alternative presentation of consolidated cash flow statement – direct method	35
Appendix III – Example disclosures for first-time adopters	36
Interim reporting disclosure checklist	63

Introduction

Objective and scope

IAS 34, 'Interim financial reporting', prescribes the minimum content for an interim financial report, and the principles for recognition and measurement, in complete and condensed financial statements for an interim period. IAS 34 was most recently amended as a consequential amendment to IAS 1 (2007), 'Presentation of financial statements' and amended by improvements to IFRS in May 2008 and IFRS 3 revised and IAS 27 revised. This resulted in changes in terminology and in the titles and layout of certain of the financial statements to be included in interim financial reports. These amendments are effective for periods beginning on or after 1 January 2009 and 1 July 2009.

There is no requirement under IFRS for entities to publish interim financial reports, but a number of territories around the world either require or recommend their publication, often stipulating that they should be prepared in accordance with IFRS. IAS 34, 'Interim financial reporting', applies where an entity publishes an interim financial report in accordance with IFRS. It encourages publicly traded entities to prepare interim reports at least as of the end of the first half of their financial year. [IAS 34 para 1].

The objective of IAS 34 is to set out the minimum content that an interim financial report should contain and the principles that should be used in recognising and measuring the transactions and balances included in that report.

IAS 34 recommends that interim financial reports are published within 60 days of the period end, although local legislative requirements may mandate a different timescale.
[IAS 34 para 1(b)].

Periods required to be presented

Based on the requirements of IAS 34 paragraph 20, the table below illustrates the statements required to be presented in the interim financial report of an entity that reports half-yearly, with a 31 December 20X0 year end.

Statements required for entities that report half-yearly

Statement	Current	Comparative
Statement of comprehensive income (and, where applicable, separate income statement) – six months ended	30 June 20X0	30 June 20X9
Balance sheet at	30 June 20X0	31 December 20X9
Statement of changes in equity – six months ended	30 June 20X0	30 June 20X9
Statement of cash flows – six months ended	30 June 20X0	30 June 20X9

First-time adoption of IFRS

IFRS 1, 'First-time adoption of International Financial Reporting Standards', applies to interim financial reports that are presented in accordance with IAS 34 for part of the period covered by the entity's first IFRS financial statements. [IFRS 1 para 2(b)]. The first IFRS interim report should contain sufficient detail to enable users to understand the effect of the transition (including the new IFRS accounting policies), as well as the IFRS 1 reconciliations between previous GAAP and IFRS. This is likely to result in a significantly longer report (see appendix III).

Auditors' review

IAS 34 and legislation do not require interim reports to be reviewed by auditors. However, the DTR require, where the management has engaged the auditor to perform a review, the auditors' interim review report to be included in the interim report.

Pro forma information

There has been increasing use of adjusted or *pro forma* information in narrative and summary disclosures in recent years. This has raised concern among regulators and users of financial statements. A particular cause for concern is where such information is presented so that it appears more representative or reliable than the numbers reported in accordance with IFRS. For example, the narrative discussion of performance may focus on strong growth in earnings before certain expenses such as one-off costs, while the statement of comprehensive income prepared in accordance with accounting standards shows a decline in profit, or even a loss. It is best practice for management to:

- make clear to the reader that any non-GAAP measures are adjusted or *pro forma*;
- reconcile non-GAAP measures to the numbers prepared in accordance with IFRS; and
- give IFRS figures greater or at least the same prominence as non-GAAP figures.

The Disclosure and Transparency Rules

The Listing Rules and the Disclosure and Transparency Rules (DTR) apply to UK companies with shares or debt listed on a regulated market. In the UK, this means principally those listed on the main market.

What impact do the DTR have on interim reporting?

The DTR set out certain requirements in relation to interim reporting. Most significantly they:

- Require a two month deadline for publication of half-yearly reports. (Online publication is sufficient.)
- Mandate that UK companies with shares or debt listed on a regulated market and that report under IFRS prepare half-yearly reports in accordance with IAS 34.
- Require the inclusion of a 'responsibility statement' by the directors.
- Require companies with listed shares to publish 'interim management statements', which need not comply with IAS 34, during the first half-year and second half-year.

Are there any exemptions available?

There are some exemptions from preparing half-yearly reports available under DTR 4.4. Issuers of wholesale debt only (denomination per unit is at least C50,000) are exempt. Issuers of retail debt (denomination per unit is less than C50,000) listed on the main market before 1 January 2005 are exempt for 10 years following 1 January 2005.

Issuers of retail debt listed on or after 1 January 2005 come under the rules.

Other exemptions from half-yearly reporting are available in relation to debt guaranteed by the State, preference shares, depository receipts, convertible securities, public sector organisations and issuers with registered offices in non-EEA states.

There are no exemptions from half-yearly reporting in the DTR for listed subsidiaries, even if a higher parent issues consolidated half-yearly reports.

Issuers of listed debt only are exempt from the requirement to prepare interim management statements (see 'Quarterly' reporting' section below), as this requirement only applies to issuers of shares.

Management commentary

IAS 34 does not require entities to present a separate management commentary; however, the DTR require a half-yearly report to include an interim management report. This should contain at least:

- An indication of important events that have occurred during the first six months of the financial year and their impact on the condensed set of financial statements; and
- A description of the principal risks and uncertainties for the remaining six months of the financial year.

The UK Listing Authority (UKLA), in the March 2008 edition of 'List!', stated that where the principal risks and uncertainties disclosed in the annual report remain valid at the half-yearly reporting date, it would be acceptable for the issuer, in its half-yearly report, to:

- State that the principal risks and uncertainties have not changed.
- Provide a summary of those principal risks and uncertainties.
- Include a cross-reference to where a detailed explanation of the principal risks and uncertainties can be found in the annual report.

If the risks and uncertainties have changed since the annual report, the new principal risks and uncertainties should be described in the interim management report.

'List!' adds that in deciding whether to include additional description, companies should consider the effect of economic turbulence and market conditions.

Additional best practice guidance on what to include in a management commentary can be found in the UK Accounting Standard Board (ASB) statement, 'Half-yearly financial reports'.

Responsibility statements

The DTR state that the directors should include a responsibility statement confirming that:

- The condensed financial statements contained in the half-yearly report give a true and fair view (this requirement can be met by stating that they are prepared in accordance with IAS 34) [DTR 4.2.10(4)]; and
- The interim management report (narrative) includes a fair review of the business and of any required related party disclosures.

The name and function of the person(s) making the statement should be disclosed. 'Person' is not defined in the DTR. However, the UKLA, in the March 2008 edition of 'List!' confirmed that, in most cases, this is expected to be either the whole board of directors or one or more directors on behalf of the board. The name and function of those responsible should be explicitly stated in the responsibility statement. This would normally be done at the end of the responsibility statement. The UKLA does not expect this information to be cross-referenced to other documents.

Printed reports are not required

Reflecting the increased use of websites, the half-yearly report does not need to be sent to shareholders or inserted as a paid advertisement in a national newspaper.

'Quarterly' reporting – interim management statements

Companies with listed shares that do not already report quarterly (either voluntarily or to meet regulatory requirements) are required to prepare interim management statements (IMS). Issuers of listed debt only are exempt from the requirement to prepare IMSs. The content requirements of an IMS are minimal and much less onerous than the original proposals that sought to bring full quarterly reporting, US-style, into the EU. The IMS should be published between 10 weeks after the beginning and six weeks before the end of the first and second six months of the period.

An IMS should provide:

- An explanation of material events and transactions and their impact on financial position; and
- A general description of financial position and performance.

The FSA has resisted issuing more prescriptive guidance on what should be included in, or could be excluded from, an IMS. It trusts issuers to use professional judgement and the market itself to develop best practice over time. The requirements are much less onerous than for half-yearly or annual reports. The IMS does not need to include any financial data. However, in practice it may be difficult to provide the necessary level of disclosure through narrative reporting only.

In some sectors in the UK, especially retail, companies are used to issuing trading updates containing mainly narrative information relating to performance, with some financial data or key performance indicators. This practice may continue. However, we believe such trading statements will need to be adapted, specifically to provide an explanation of material events and transactions (such as acquisitions, disposals, new strategies, markets and products and operational disruption) and a description of financial position (for example, adequacy of financing and working capital to service acquisition plans and capital expenditure).

Do the DTR apply to AIM companies too?

AIM-listed companies are required to report under IFRS, but they do not come under the requirement to issue IAS 34-compliant interims. The DTR apply to UK companies with shares or debt listed on a regulated market. AIM is not classed as a 'regulated market' under EU Law but an 'exchange regulated market'. AIM companies are not therefore subject to the DTR and should apply the AIM rules.

AIM rule 18 requires AIM-listed companies to produce a half-yearly report but does not mandate the use of IAS 34. They therefore have the choice of whether to prepare half-yearly reports under IAS 34 or to comply with the minimum disclosures in AIM rule 18. They should be mindful of best practice guidance on the content of interims reports.

Is there guidance for UK GAAP reporters?

The ASB's Statement, 'Half-yearly financial reports' is consistent with all major aspects of IAS 34 and the DTR, including terminology.

The DTR make the ASB's Statement mandatory for UK-listed companies not issuing interim reports under IAS 34 – for example, solus companies with no subsidiaries that still report under UK GAAP. Other UK GAAP reporters – for example, unlisted companies that choose to voluntarily issue half-yearly reports – are encouraged to use the guidance in the ASB's Statement.

The ASB's Statement is similar to the requirements of IAS 34, but there are a number of differences. For example:

- The ASB's Statement does not require the extensive quantitative disclosures of business combinations required by IAS 34; a narrative commentary containing details of acquisitions and disposals should be given.
- The ASB's Statement requires segment information consistent with that to be used at the year-end, where possible. Where not possible, that fact should be stated along with an explanation as to why.
- The ASB's Statement is silent on related-party transactions. However, listed companies subject to the DTR that do not prepare consolidated accounts should give details of related-party transactions, amounts, and the nature of the relationship, for material transactions not concluded under normal market conditions.

- The periods to be presented differ from those required by IAS 34. The ASB's Statement requires income statement, statement of total recognised gains and losses and cash flow statement comparatives for the corresponding interim period and the preceding full year. There is no requirement to report year-to-date information (primarily because there is no requirement for quarterly reporting).

The auditors' review report

The Auditing Practices Board's 'Statement of standards for reporting accountants', ISRE (UK and Ireland) 2410, 'Review of interim financial information performed by the independent auditor of the entity', includes an example review report for use in the UK.

If an auditors' review or audit report comes under the Auditing Practices Board guidance on the review of interim financial information, the DTR require this to be reproduced in full. If the interim report has not been audited or reviewed, the DTR require a statement to this effect.

What are the top 10 interim reporting pitfalls?

Our experiences of reviewing interim reports suggest that the following errors or omissions are the most frequent:

- Principal risks and uncertainties not disclosed.
- Name and function of persons making the responsibility statement not given (or responsibility statement omitted entirely).
- Incorrect or no disclosure of new standards, amendments and IFRIC interpretations.
- Basis of preparation note incorrect (for example, does not refer to IAS 34, the DTR or IFRSs as adopted by the European Union).
- Omission of the nature and amount of items that are unusual by their nature, size or incidence.
- Omission of some or all business combinations disclosures, especially those related to combinations after the interim reporting date.
- Omission of details of material property, plant and equipment acquired or disposed of during the period.
- Omission of details of material changes in estimates – for example, relating to provisions, defined benefit pension obligations and impairments.
- No explanations of the effect of seasonality on operations.
- Statement of comprehensive income includes incorrect entries or omits correct entries.

Illustrative interim financial information for the half-year ended 30 June 2010

This illustrative condensed consolidated interim financial information is prepared in accordance with IAS 34, 'Interim financial reporting', as adopted by the European Union and the FSA's Disclosure and Transparency Rules (DTR).

The company (VALUE ACCOUNTS Holdings) manufactures and sells high-quality household and commercial office furniture. It provides IT consulting, including IT management, design, implementation and support. The Group is also involved in the development and resale of land and the management of investment properties. VALUE ACCOUNTS Holdings is an existing preparer of IFRS consolidated financial statements; IFRS 1, 'First-time adoption of International Financial Reporting Standards', is not applicable. VALUE ACCOUNTS Holdings is an issuer of shares and does not have listed debt. It is domiciled in the UK.

The IFRS standards and IFRIC interpretations considered in preparing this illustrative interim financial information are those issued by the IASB up to 31 March 2010 that are mandatory for the year end 31 December 2010. New presentations and disclosures have been highlighted in grey.

We have attempted to create realistic condensed consolidated interim financial information for a corporate entity. Certain types of transaction have not been included, as they are not relevant to the Group's operations.

The example disclosures are not the only acceptable form of presentation. The form and content of each reporting entity's condensed consolidated interim financial information is the responsibility of the entity's management. Any form of presentation may be adopted, if it complies with the specific disclosure requirements prescribed in IAS 34.

This illustrative condensed consolidated interim financial information is not a substitute for reading the standards and interpretations themselves or for professional judgement as to fairness of presentation. It does not cover all possible disclosures that IAS 34 requires.

Format of the publication

The references in the left-hand margin refer to the paragraph of the standard in which the disclosure appears, for example, '34p11' indicates IAS 34 paragraph 11. The reference to IFRS appears in full, for example, 'IFRS3p67' indicates IFRS 3 paragraph 67. References to the Disclosure and Transparency Rules appear as, for example, DTR 4.2.3. References to the Companies Act 2006 section 435, for example, appear as CA06 s435(1). The designation 'DV' (disclosure voluntary) indicates that disclosure is encouraged but not required.

PricewaterhouseCoopers commentary

These illustrative interim financial statements are a guide to IAS 34 and should be used in conjunction with the supporting commentary on interim reporting requirements set out below.

Commentary – notes to the consolidated financial statements

Minimum note disclosures

34p16 1. As a minimum, an entity should include the information set out in paragraph 16 of IAS 34 in the notes in the interim financial report, unless the information is not material or disclosed elsewhere in the interim financial report. The information should normally be reported on an annual-reporting-period-to-date basis.

34p15 2. In addition, the entity should disclose any events or transactions that are material to an understanding of the current interim period. In May 2009, the IFRIC noted that an interim financial report provides an update on the latest complete set of annual financial statements. Therefore, when an event or transaction is significant to an understanding of the changes in an entity's financial position or performance since the last annual financial period, the interim financial report should provide an explanation of, and update to, the information included in the financial statements for the last annual financial period.

3. Examples of events that may require additional disclosures are:
   - (a) the impact of the adoption of a new standard;
   - (b) the impact of the future adoption of a standard that has been issued but does not yet need to be applied by the entity – in particular, where this could have a significant impact such as the adoption of IFRS 9, 'Financial instruments';
   - (c) a deterioration of the credit exposures reported in the annual financial statements that resulted in the accounting for losses that are unusual because of their nature, size or incidence;
   - (d) the fact that certain financial instruments have ceased to be traded in an active market during the interim period and that a valuation technique has been used to measure their fair value;
   - (e) the use of different valuation techniques compared to those utilised for the amounts included in the annual results;
   - (f) a significant change in the financial risk management approach of the entity. This would be disclosed under IFRS 7 if the quantitative disclosures of the entity's exposure to financial risks and its sensitivity to market risks reported at the end of the annual financial period is not representative of its exposure and sensitivity during the interim period; and
   - (g) the reclassification of financial instruments out of the fair value through profit or loss category under the circumstances outlined in paragraph 50B of IAS 39.

Accounting policies

34p16(a) 4. The interim financial report should include a statement that the same accounting policies and methods of computation are followed in the interim financial report as compared with the most recent annual financial statements or, if those policies or methods have been changed, a description of the nature and effect of the change.

5. Where an entity prepares its first interim financial report and there is no previous annual report, we believe that a complete disclosure of significant accounting policies should be provided.

Segment information

34p16(g) 6. IAS 34 requires disclosure of segment information if an entity is within the scope of IFRS 8, 'Segment reporting'. This includes:

(a) the following amounts, if they are included in the measure of segment profit or loss reviewed by the chief operating decision-maker or otherwise regularly provided to the chief operating decision-maker:
   (i) revenues from external customers;
   (ii) intersegment revenues; and
(b) a measure of segment profit or loss;
(c) total assets for which there has been a material change from the amount disclosed in the last annual financial statements;
(d) a description of the differences from the last annual financial statements in the basis of segmentation or in the basis of measurement of segment profit or loss;
(e) a reconciliation of the total of the reportable segment measures of profit or loss to the entity's profit or loss before tax expense (tax income) and discontinued operations (this can be done on an after-tax basis if tax is allocated to reportable segments)

Unusual items

34p16(c) 7. Disclosure is required of the nature and amount of items affecting assets, liabilities, equity, profit or loss, or cash flows that are unusual because of their nature, size or incidence.

34p17 8. Examples listed in IAS 34 of items that may be required to be separately disclosed are:

(a) a write-down of inventories to net realisable value and the reversal of such a write-down;
(b) recognition of a loss from the impairment of property, plant and equipment, intangible assets, or other assets, and the reversal of such an impairment loss;
(c) the reversal of any provisions for the costs of restructuring;
(d) acquisitions and disposals of items of property, plant and equipment;
(e) commitments for the purchase of property, plant, and equipment;
(f) litigation settlements;
(g) corrections of prior period errors;
(h) any loan default or breach of a loan agreement that has not been remedied on or before the end of the reporting period; and
(i) related-party transactions.

9. IAS 34 does not require disclosure of the income tax applicable to unusual items. However, we recommend its disclosure in interim reports in the absence of detailed income tax note disclosures.

Changes in the composition of the entity

34p16(i) 10. IAS 34 requires interim financial reports to disclose the effect of changes in the composition of the entity during the interim period, including business combinations, obtaining or losing control of subsidiaries and long-term investments, restructurings, and discontinued operations. In the case of business combinations, the entity should disclose the information required to be disclosed under paragraphs 59-62 and B64-B67 of IFRS 3, 'Business combinations'.

Comparative information for narrative disclosures

11. IAS 34 does not comment on whether narrative information that was disclosed in the interim financial report for the comparative period should be repeated in the current interim financial report. However, as per paragraph 6 of IAS 34, the interim

financial report is intended to provide an update on the last complete set of annual financial statements. It should therefore focus on new activities, events and circumstances; it does not need to duplicate information previously reported. On this basis, we do not believe it is necessary to repeat business combination disclosures that were also included in the latest annual financial statements. However, we have chosen to retain the comparative disclosures for the discontinued operation, as this disclosure explains amounts separately presented in the income statement for the comparative period. These amounts might not be the same as the amounts reported in relation to the discontinued operation in the latest annual financial statements.

Contingent liabilities

34p16(j) 12. The interim financial report should disclose changes in contingent liabilities or contingent assets since the end of the last annual reporting period.

Events occurring after the reporting period

34p16(h) 13. The interim financial report should disclose material events subsequent to the end of the interim period that have not been reflected in the interim financial statements. Such disclosure normally includes an indication of the financial effect of each event, where possible.

Disclosures not illustrated: not applicable to VALUE ACCOUNTS Holdings

Changes in estimates

34p16(d) 14. The interim financial report should disclose the nature and amount of changes in estimates of amounts reported in prior interim periods of the current annual reporting period or changes in estimates of amounts reported in prior annual reporting periods, if those changes have a material effect in the current interim period.

Issuances, repurchases and repayments of debt and equity securities

34p16(e) 15. The interim financial report should disclose details of issuances, repurchases and repayments of debt and equity securities. Repurchases and repayments of equity securities are not illustrated in the disclosures in this example interim report because there were no such transactions during the half-year under review.

Business combinations

16. In addition to the disclosures illustrated in note 12, entities should also disclose information about the following items where applicable:

IFRS3B64(j) (a) contingent liabilities (at acquisition and subsequently);

IFRS3 B64(l),(m) (b) transactions that are recognised separately from the business combinations, including acquisition-related costs;

IFRS3 B64(n) (c) bargain purchases;

IFRS 3B64(p) (d) business combinations achieved in stages;

IFRS 3B67(a) (e) incomplete initial accounting for a business combination and subsequent adjustments;

IFRS 3B67(b) (f) changes to contingent consideration assets and liabilities; and

IFRS 3B67(e) (g) gains and losses recognised during the period relating to assets or liabilities acquired in a business combination in the current or previous reporting period.

VALUE ACCOUNTS Holdings
Interim financial information (unaudited)

30 June 2010

Contents

	Page
Interim management report	13
Consolidated income statement	15
Consolidated statement of comprehensive income	16
Consolidated balance sheet	17
Consolidated statement of changes in equity	18
Consolidated statement of cash flows	19
Notes to the consolidated interim financial statements	20
Statement of directors' responsibility	31
Auditors' review report	32

Interim management report

34p8(e) VALUE ACCOUNTS Holdings manufactures and sells high-quality household and commercial office furniture. It provides IT consulting, including IT management, design, implementation and support. The Group is also involved in the development and resale of land and the management of investment properties. The Group has operations mainly in countries within the eurozone, the US and UK.

DTR 4.2.7(1)

Key events

34p8(e) The operational highlight of the period was the acquisition of Office Furnishings Company A, a company that manufactures office furniture and equipment. Further details are given in Note 12.

In June 2010, the Group renegotiated its existing loan facility to finance the construction of the new production plant for the electronic equipment division. Further details are given in Note 8.

A new legal claim was brought against the Group in May 2010, asserting that the IT consulting division had breached certain registered patents of a competitor. Further details are given in Note 7.

On 1 August 2010, VALUE ACCOUNTS Holdings acquired all of the issued shares in Office Furniture C, a manufacturer and retailer of premium office furniture and equipment. Further details are given in Note 15.

Performance

Furniture – manufacturing

The furniture and manufacturing division manufactures and sells a range of furniture, principally hardwood side-boards, chairs and tables and commercial office furniture. The division was adversely affected by new competitors in Eastern Europe; however, this was countered in the 2009 financial year by the development of additional business in the UK, which has continued in this half year, and the profit of C670,000 (C469,000 after tax) on the sale of freehold land.

Operating profit increased by 37% to C4.8 million (2009: C3.5 million) on the corresponding period, reflecting strong cost control and more favourable contract pricing structures with four principal raw materials suppliers.

Position

The Group had cash at the half-year of C9.3 million (2009: C8.2 million). The increase in the cash balance reflects an increase in cash flows from the strong sale of electronic equipment. The Group has sufficient working capital and undrawn financing facilities to service its operating activities.

DTR 4.2.7(2)

Principal risks and uncertainties

The Group set out in its 2009 Annual Report and Financial Statements the principal risks and uncertainties that could impact its performance; these remain unchanged since the Annual Report was published. The Group operates a structured risk management process, which identifies and evaluates risks and uncertainties and reviews mitigation activity.

The past six months have seen a gradual improvement in financial market conditions. This has resulted in an overall improvement in the risk environment. The Group remains well placed to increase revenues through ongoing product innovation and the recent acquisition of Office Furnishings Company A. The Group has no exposure to sub-prime lending or collateralised debt obligations. The Group has sufficient headroom to enable it to conform to covenants on its existing borrowings. The Group has sufficient working capital and undrawn financing facilities to service its operating activities.

The Group should be able to realise the significant synergies arising from the acquisition of Office Furnishings Company A. The acquisition is expected to increase the Group's market share and reduce cost through economies of sale.

The main area of potential risk and uncertainty on a short-term forward-looking basis over the remainder of the financial year centres on the sales and profit impact from economic conditions and consumer demand, together with the impact of product cost pressures, particularly as a result of sterling weakness, and an associated level of customer price inflation. Other potential risks and uncertainties around sales and/or profits include competitor activity, product supply and other operational processes, product safety, business interruption, infrastructure development, reliance on key personnel, and the regulatory environment. These risks, together with examples of mitigating activity, are set out in more detail in the 2009 Annual Report and Financial Statements on pages 24 and 28, available on VALUE ACCOUNTS Holdings website: www.valueifrs.com.

Related parties

DTR 4.2.8 Related-party disclosures are given in Note 14.

Forward-looking statements

DV (ASB Reporting Statement OFR para 10) Certain statements in this interim report are forward-looking. Although the Group believes that the expectations reflected in these forward-looking statements are reasonable, it can give no assurance that these expectations will prove to have been correct. Because these statements involve risks and uncertainties, actual results may differ materially from those expressed or implied by these forward-looking statements.

The Group undertakes no obligation to update any forward-looking statements whether as a result of new information, future events or otherwise.

(All amounts in C thousands unless otherwise stated)

Consolidated income statement

34p8(b), 34p10, 34p20(b)

	Notes	Half-year 2010	2009
Continuing operations			
Revenue		**32,100**	26,174
Cost of sales		**(24,153)**	(19,669)
Gross profit		**7,947**	6,505
Distribution costs		**(833)**	(697)
Administrative expenses		**(2,307)**	(2,293)
Operating profit		**4,807**	3,515
Finance income		**1**	1
Finance costs		**(788)**	(609)
Share of post tax profits of associates and joint venture		**205**	340
Profit before income tax		**4,225**	3,247
Income tax expense		**(1,175)**	(909)
Profit from continuing operations		**3,050**	2,338
Discontinued operations			
Profit from discontinued operations	11	**–**	715
Profit for the half-year		**3,050**	3,053
Profit is attributable to:			
– Owners of VALUE ACCOUNTS Holdings		**2,600**	2,565
– Non-controlling interests		**450**	488
		3,050	3,053

		Cents per share	**Cents per share**
34p11	**Earnings per share for profit attributable to the ordinary equity holders of the company**		
	– Basic earnings per share	**18.8**	22.0
	– Diluted earnings per share	**18.0**	21.5
	Earnings per share for profit from continuing operations attributable to the ordinary equity holders of the company		
	– Basic earnings per share	**18.8**	15.9
	– Diluted earnings per share	**18.0**	15.5

The above consolidated income statement should be read in conjunction with the accompanying notes.

(All amounts in C thousands unless otherwise stated)

Consolidated statement of comprehensive income

34p20(b)

	Notes	Half-year 2010	2009
Profit for the half-year		**3,050**	3,053
Other comprehensive income			
Gain on revaluation of land and buildings		**195**	260
Changes in the fair value of available-for-sale financial assets		**16**	14
Changes in the fair value of derivatives held as cash flow hedges		**284**	18
Actuarial gains/(losses) on retirement benefit obligation		**81**	(143)
Net investment hedge		**4**	–
Exchange differences on translation of foreign operations		**(5)**	15
Income tax relating to components of other comprehensive income		**(172)**	(44)
Other comprehensive income for the half-year, net of tax		**403**	120
Total comprehensive income for the half-year		**3,453**	3,173
Total comprehensive income for the half-year is attributable to:			
Owners of VALUE ACCOUNTS Holdings		**3,003**	2,685
Non-controlling interests		**450**	488
		3,453	3,173

The above consolidated income statement should be read in conjunction with the accompanying notes.

(All amounts in C thousands unless otherwise stated)

Consolidated balance sheet

34p8(a), 34p10
34p20(a), DTR
4.2.3(1)

	Notes	30 June 2010	31 December 2009
Assets			
Non-current assets			
Property, plant and equipment	6	**13,535**	12,095
Investment properties		**3,150**	3,300
Intangible assets		**1,512**	865
Investments accounted for using the equity method		**3,680**	3,775
Available-for-sale financial assets		**1,060**	1,010
Held-to-maturity investments		**300**	210
Derivative financial instruments		**10**	8
Deferred tax assets		**1,112**	734
Receivables		**1,530**	1,476
Total non-current assets		**25,889**	23,473
Current assets			
Inventories		**6,780**	7,153
Trade and other receivables		**12,427**	12,935
Financial assets at fair value through profit or loss		**1,150**	1,300
Derivative financial instruments		**68**	88
Cash and cash equivalents		**9,308**	8,229
		29,733	29,705
Assets classified as held for sale		–	250
Total current assets		**29,733**	29,955
Total assets		**55,622**	53,428
Liabilities			
Non-current liabilities			
Borrowings	8	**10,225**	9,464
Deferred tax liabilities		**1,640**	1,289
Provisions		**442**	443
Retirement benefit obligations		**377**	482
Total non-current liabilities		**12,684**	11,678
Current liabilities			
Trade and other payables		**1,725**	1,700
Borrowings		**2,590**	2,980
Derivative financial instruments		**270**	310
Current tax liabilities		**1,202**	2,746
Provisions	7	**635**	360
Other liabilities		**350**	395
Total current liabilities		**6,772**	8,491
Total liabilities		**19,456**	20,169
Net assets		**36,166**	33,259
Equity			
Share capital		**19,504**	18,990
Reserves		**1,588**	1,385
Retained earnings		**11,874**	10,199
Capital and reserves attributable to the owners of VALUE ACCOUNTS Holdings		**32,966**	30,574
Non-controlling interests		**3,200**	2,685
Total equity		**36,166**	33,259

The above consolidated balance sheet should be read in conjunction with the accompanying notes.

(All amounts in C thousands unless otherwise stated)

Consolidated statement of changes in equity

34p8(c)
34p20(c)
34p10, DTR 4.2.3(1)

		Attributable to owners of VALUE ACCOUNTS Holdings					
Consolidated	**Notes**	**Share capital**	**Reserves**	**Retained earnings**	**Total**	**Non-controlling interests**	**Total equity**
Balance at 1 January 2009		**13,870**	**636**	**4,184**	**18,690**	**1,596**	**20,286**
Total comprehensive income for the half-year		**–**	**213**	**2,472**	**2,685**	**488**	**3,173**
Transactions with owners in their capacity as owners:							
– Contributions of equity, net of transaction costs	9	162	–	–	162	–	162
– Non-controlling interest on acquisition of subsidiary		–	–	–	–	575	575
– Dividends provided for or paid	10	–	–	(586)	(586)	(109)	(695)
– Employee share options – value of employee services		–	47	–	47	–	47
– Employee share scheme		–	7	–	7	–	7
		162	54	(586)	(370)	466	96
Balance at 30 June 2009		**14,032**	**903**	**6,070**	**21,005**	**2,550**	**23,555**
34p20(c) **Balance at 1 January 2010**		**19,200**	**1,175**	**10,199**	**30,574**	**2,685**	**33,259**
Total comprehensive income for the half-year		**–**	**339**	**2,664**	**3,003**	**450**	**3,453**
Transactions with owners in their capacity as owners:							
– Contributions of equity, net of transaction costs	9	304	–	–	304	–	304
– Non-controlling interest on acquisition of subsidiary		–	–	–	–	250	250
– Dividends provided for or paid	10	–	–	(989)	(989)	(185)	(1,174)
– Employee share options – value of employee services		–	63	–	63	–	63
– Employee share scheme		–	11	–	11	–	11
		304	74	(989)	(611)	65	(546)
Balance at 30 June 2010		**19,504**	**1,588**	**11,874**	**32,966**	**3,200**	**36,166**

The above consolidated statement of changes in equity should be read in conjunction with the accompanying notes.

(All amounts in C thousands unless otherwise stated)

Consolidated statement of cash flows[1]

34p8(d), 34p10, 34p20(d)

		Notes	Half-year 2010	2009
	Cash flows from operating activities			
	Cash generated from operations		**8,899**	754
	Interest paid		**(893)**	(603)
	Income taxes paid		**(2,937)**	(1,147)
	Net cash inflow (outflow) from operating activities		**5,069**	(996)
	Cash flows from investing activities:			
	– acquisition of subsidiary, net of cash acquired	12	**(3,575)**	(1,500)
	– property, plant and equipment	6	**(2,060)**	(2,511)
	– investment property		**–**	(150)
	– available-for-sale financial assets		**(73)**	(27)
	– held-to-maturity investments		**(83)**	(180)
	– patents and trademarks		**(20)**	(9)
	– development costs		**(25)**	(58)
	– sale of machinery hire division	11	**–**	3,960
	– sale of property, plant and equipment		**2,425**	1,495
	– sale of available-for-sale financial assets		**49**	85
	Joint venture partnership distributions received		**250**	120
	Dividends received		**160**	150
	Interest received		**170**	180
	Net cash (outflow) inflow from investing activities		**(2,782)**	1,555
	Cash flows from financing activities:			
34p16(e)	– issues of shares and other equity securities	9	**104**	–
34p16(e)	– borrowings	8	**6,487**	4,500
	– shares acquired by the VALUE ACCOUNTS Employee Share Trust	9	**(459)**	(450)
34p16(e)	Repayment of borrowings		**(6,050)**	(3,400)
34p16(e)	Finance lease payments		**(16)**	(25)
34p16(f)	Dividends paid to company's shareholders		**(784)**	(412)
	Dividends paid to non-controlling interests in subsidiaries		**(185)**	(110)
	Net cash inflow (outflow) from financing activities		**(903)**	103
	Net increase (decrease) in cash and cash equivalents		**1,384**	662
	Cash and cash equivalents at the beginning of the half-year		**5,879**	562
	Effects of exchange rate changes on cash and cash equivalents		**5**	(7)
	Cash and cash equivalents at end of the half-year		**7,268**	1,217

The above consolidated statement of cash flows should be read in conjunction with the accompanying notes.

[1] We have presented cash flows from operating activities using the indirect method. An example statement of cash flows presenting operating cash flows using the direct method is in Appendix II.

(All amounts in C thousands unless otherwise stated)

Notes to the consolidated interim financial statements

1 General information

34p8(e) The Company is a limited liability company incorporated and domiciled in One-land. The address of its registered office is Nice Walk Way, Runningville.

The Company has its primary listing on the EuroMoney Stock Exchange.

This condensed consolidated interim financial information was approved for issue on 24 August 2010.

CA06 s435(1) This condensed consolidated interim financial information does not comprise statutory accounts within the meaning of section 434 of the Companies Act 2006. Statutory accounts for the year ended 31 December 2009 were approved by the Board of directors on 17 April 2010 and delivered to the Registrar of Companies. The report of the auditors on those accounts was unqualified, did not contain an emphasis of matter paragraph and did not contain any statement under section 498 of the Companies Act 2006.

This consolidated interim financial information has been reviewed, not audited[2].

2 Basis of preparation of half-year report

34p19 This condensed consolidated interim financial information for the half-year ended 30 June 2010 has been prepared in accordance with the Disclosure and Transparency Rules of the Financial Services Authority and with IAS 34, 'Interim financial reporting', as adopted by the European Union. The condensed consolidated interim financial information should be read in conjunction with the annual financial statements for the year ended 31 December 2009, which have been prepared in accordance with IFRSs as adopted by the European Union.

3 Accounting policies

34p28, 34p16(a) The accounting policies are consistent with those of the annual financial statements for the year ended 31 December 2009, except as described below.

34pB12 Taxes on income in the interim periods are accrued using the tax rate that would be applicable to expected total annual earnings.

(a) New and amended standards adopted by the Group

The following new standards and amendments to standards are mandatory for the first time for the financial year beginning 1 January 2010.

IFRS 3 (revised), 'Business combinations', and consequential amendments to IAS 27, 'Consolidated and separate financial statements', IAS 28, 'Investments in associates', and IAS 31, 'Interests in joint ventures', are effective prospectively to business combinations for which the acquisition date is on or after the beginning of the first annual reporting period beginning on or after 1 July 2009.

[2] Local legislation may require interim financial information to be reviewed or audited.

(All amounts in C thousands unless otherwise stated)

The revised standard continues to apply the acquisition method to business combinations but with some significant changes compared with IFRS 3. For example, all payments to purchase a business are recorded at fair value at the acquisition date, with contingent payments classified as debt subsequently re-measured through the income statement. There is a choice on an acquisition-by-acquisition basis to measure the non-controlling interest in the acquiree either at fair value or at the non-controlling interest's proportionate share of the acquiree's net assets. All acquisition-related costs are expensed.

As the Group has adopted IFRS 3 (revised), it is required to adopt IAS 27 (revised), 'consolidated and separate financial statements', at the same time. IAS 27 (revised) requires the effects of all transactions with non-controlling interests to be recorded in equity if here is no change in control and these transactions will no longer result in goodwill or gains and losses. The standard also specifies the accounting when control is lost. Any remaining interest in the entity is re-measured to fair value, and a gain or loss is recognised in profit or loss. There has been no impact of IAS 27 (revised) on the current period, as none of the non-controlling interests have a deficit balance. There have been no transactions whereby an interest in an entity is retained after the loss of control of that entity; there have been no transactions with non-controlling interests.

(b) Standards, amendments and interpretations to existing standards effective in 2010 but not relevant to the Group

- IFRIC 17, 'Distributions of non-cash assets to owners', effective for annual periods beginning on or after 1 July 2009. This is not currently applicable to the Group, as it has not made any non-cash distributions.
- IFRIC 18, 'Transfers of assets from customers', effective for transfer of assets received on or after 1 July 2009. This is not relevant to the Group, as it has not received any assets from customers.
- 'Additional exemptions for first-time adopters' (Amendment to IFRS 1) was issued in July 2009. The amendments are required to be applied for annual periods beginning on or after 1 January 2010. This is not relevant to the Group, as it is an existing IFRS preparer.
- Improvements to International Financial Reporting Standards 2009 were issued in April 2009. The effective dates vary standard by standard but most are effective 1 January 2010.

DV *(c) The following new standards, new interpretations and amendments to standards and interpretations have been issued but are not effective for the financial year beginning 1 January 2010 and have not been early adopted:*

- IFRS 9, 'Financial instruments', issued in December 2009. This addresses the classification and measurement of financial assets and is likely to affect the Group's accounting for its financial assets. The standard is not applicable until 1 January 2013 but is available for early adoption. The Group is yet to assess IFRS 9's full impact. However, initial indications are that it may affect the Group's accounting for its available-for-sale financial assets, as IFRS 9 only permits the recognition of fair value gains and losses in other comprehensive income if they relate to equity investments that are not held for trading. Fair value gains and losses on available-for-sale debt investments, for example, will therefore have to be recognised directly in profit or loss. In the current reporting period, the Group recognised C5,000 of such gains in other comprehensive income. The Group has not yet decided when to adopt IFRS 9.

(All amounts in C thousands unless otherwise stated)

- Revised IAS 24, 'Related party disclosures', issued in November 2009. It supersedes IAS 24, 'Related party disclosures', issued in 2003. The revised IAS 24 is required to be applied from 1 January 2011. Earlier application, in whole or in part, is permitted.
- 'Classification of rights issues' (Amendment to IAS 32), issued in October 2009. For rights issues offered for a fixed amount of foreign currency, current practice appears to require such issues to be accounted for as derivative liabilities. The amendment states that if such rights are issued pro rata to all the entity's existing shareholders in the same class for a fixed amount of currency, they should be classified as equity regardless of the currency in which the exercise price is denominated. The amendment should be applied for annual periods beginning on or after 1 February 2010. Earlier application is permitted.
- 'Prepayments of a minimum funding requirement' (Amendments to IFRIC 14), issued in November 2009. The amendments correct an unintended consequence of IFRIC 14, 'IAS 19 – The limit on a defined benefit asset, minimum funding requirements and their interaction'. Without the amendments, entities are not permitted to recognise as an asset some voluntary prepayments for minimum funding contributions. This was not intended when IFRIC 14 was issued, and the amendments correct the problem. The amendments are effective for annual periods beginning 1 January 2011. Earlier application is permitted. The amendments should be applied retrospectively to the earliest comparative period presented.
- IFRIC 19, 'Extinguishing financial liabilities with equity instruments'. This clarifies the requirements of IFRSs when an entity renegotiates the terms of a financial liability with its creditor and the creditor agrees to accept the entity's shares or other equity instruments to settle the financial liability fully or partially. The interpretation is effective for annual periods beginning on or after 1 July 2010. Earlier application is permitted.
- Improvements to International Financial Reporting Standards 2010 were issued in May 2010. The effective dates vary standard by standard but most are effective 1 January 2010.

Seasonality of operations

34p16(b) Due to the seasonal nature of the electronics segment, higher revenues and operating profits are usually expected in the second half of the year than in the first six months.

4 Segment information

34p16(g)(v) *(a) Description of segments*

Management has determined the operating segments based on the reports reviewed by the strategic steering committee that are used to make strategic decisions. The strategic steering committee currently consists of the managing director, the chief financial officer and the manager for corporate planning.

The committee considers the business from both a product and a geographic perspective and has identified six reportable segments. Furniture manufacturing consists of commercial office furniture, hardwood side boards, chairs and tables, which are manufactured and sold in the UK and in the US. The committee monitors the performance in those two regions separately. Since January 2009, the manufacturing business has been supplemented by a chain of retail stores in the UK (the furniture retail segment). The IT consulting segment consists of business IT management, and design, implementation and support services. All are provided in the UK and in a number of Eastern European countries. Performance is also monitored separately for those two regions.

(All amounts in C thousands unless otherwise stated)

Although the electronic equipment segment does not meet the quantitative thresholds required by IFRS 8, management has concluded that this segment should be reported, as it is closely monitored by the strategic steering committee as a potential growth segment and is expected to materially contribute to group revenue in the future. This segment was established following the acquisition of VALUE ACCOUNTS Electronics UK Ltd in April 2009.

The development of residential land – currently in Suburb A in London and Suburb B in Edinburgh – the purchase and resale of commercial properties – principally in Manchester and Bristol – and the management of investment properties are not reportable operating segments, as they are not separately included in the reports provided to the strategic steering committee. The results of these operations are included in the 'all other segments' column.

The machinery-hire division was sold effective from 1 March 2009. Information about this discontinued segment is provided in note 11.

IFRS 8p23 *(b) Segment information provided to the strategic steering committee*

The segment information provided to the strategic steering committee for the reportable segments for the half-year ended 30 June 2010 is as follows:

		Furniture – manufacture		Furniture – retail	IT consulting		Electronic equipment		Total
	Half-year 2010	**UK**	**US**	**UK**	**UK**	**Eastern Europe**	**UK**	**All other segments**	
34p16(g)(i)	Total segment revenue	9,700	2,165	5,290	9,810	2,370	1,800	2,165	33,300
34p16(g)(ii)	Inter-segment revenue	(50)	(50)	(400)	(200)	(100)	(200)	(200)	(1,200)
	Revenue from external customers	9,650	2,115	4,890	9,610	2,270	1,600	1,965	32,100
34p16(g)(iii)	**Adjusted EBITDA**	1,645	534	1,403	702	480	330	370	5,464
	Half-year 2009								
34p16(g)(i)	Total segment revenue	8,434	2,200	3,422	8,459	2,000	1,449	1,560	27,524
34p16(g)(ii)	Inter-segment revenue	(50)	(100)	(300)	(200)	(100)	(300)	(300)	(1,350)
	Revenue from external customers	8,384	2,100	3,122	8,259	1,900	1,149	1,260	26,174
34p16(g)(iii)	**Adjusted EBITDA**	1,343	403	710	1,301	450	260	394	4,861
34p16(g)(iv)	**Total segment assets 30 June 2010**	12,049	5,700	11,910	9,970	3,815	2,225	6,380	52,049
	31 December 2009	11,830	5,500	11,600	9,640	3,500	2,090	6,218	50,378

(All amounts in C thousands unless otherwise stated)

The strategic steering committee assesses the performance of the operating segments based on a measure of adjusted EBITDA. This measurement basis excludes the effects of non-recurring expenditure from the operating segments, such as restructuring costs, legal expenses and goodwill impairments when the impairment is the result of an isolated, non-recurring event. The measure excludes the effects of equity-settled share-based payments and unrealised gains/losses on financial instruments. Interest income and expenditure are not allocated to segments, as this type of activity is driven by the central treasury function, which manages the cash position of the Group.

34p16(g)(vi) A reconciliation of adjusted EBITDA to profit before income tax is provided as follows:

	2010	2009
Adjusted EBITDA – for reportable segments	**5,094**	4,467
Other segments – EBITDA	**370**	394
Total segments	**5,464**	4,861
Intersegment eliminations	**(45)**	(30)
Interest revenue	**175**	150
Net finance costs	**(787)**	(608)
Depreciation and amortisation expense	**(833)**	(697)
Legal expenses	**–**	(300)
Unrealised financial instrument gains/(losses)	**325**	(75)
Share options granted to directors and employees	**(74)**	(54)
Profit before income tax and discontinued operations	**4,225**	3,247

The amounts provided to the strategic steering committee with respect to total assets are measured in a manner consistent with that of the financial statements. These assets are allocated based on the operations of the segment and the physical location of the asset.

5 Profit for the half-year

Profit for the half-year includes the following items, which are unusual because of their nature, size or incidence:

		Half-year	
		2010	2009
	Gains		
34p16(c)	Gain on sale of freehold land	–	670
DV	Less: Applicable income tax expense	–	(201)
		–	469
	Expenses		
34p16(c)	Provision for legal claim – see note 7 below	**375**	–
DV	Less: Applicable income tax	**(113)**	–
		262	–
34p16(c)	Impairment of goodwill	–	410
DV	Less: Applicable income tax benefit	–	–
		–	410

(All amounts in C thousands unless otherwise stated)

34p16(c)	Write-off of assets destroyed by fire:		
	– Office and warehouse building	–	465
	– Plant and equipment	–	210
	– Inventories	–	535
		–	1,210
	Less: Insurance recovery	–	(300)
		–	910
DV	Less: Applicable income tax benefit	–	(273)
		–	637

6 Property, plant and equipment

34p16(c), p17(d) In June 2010, the Group acquired a block of vacant land in Edinburgh at a cost of C1,700,000. The land will be used for the construction of additional production facilities for the electronic equipment division.

7 Current provisions

34p16(c) A new legal claim was brought against the Group in May 2010. A provision of C375,000 was recognised for this claim.

8 Non-current borrowings

34p16(c), (e) In June 2010, the Group renegotiated its existing loan facility to finance the construction of the new production plant for the electronic equipment division. The total available amount under the facility was increased by C2,000,000, of which C700,000 was drawn down as at 30 June 2010. The full facility is now repayable in three annual instalments, commencing 1 June 2016.

The loan is a fixed rate, C-denominated loan, which is carried at amortised cost. The renegotiation did not therefore have any impact on the Group's exposure to foreign exchange and interest rate risk. As at 30 June 2010, the contractual maturities of the Group's non-derivative financial liabilities were as follows:

Contractual maturities of financial liabilities	Less than 6 months	6-12 months	Between 1 and 2 years	Between 2 and 5 years	Over 5 years	Total contractual cash flows	Carrying amount (assets)/ liabilities
At 30 June 2010							
Non-derivatives							
Trade payables	1,725	–	–	–	–	1,725	1,725
Borrowings (excluding finance leases)	1,439	1,300	500	2,490	7,761	13,490	12,300
Finance lease liabilities	61	61	120	355	95	692	515
Total non-derivatives	**3,225**	**1,361**	**620**	**2,845**	**7,856**	**15,907**	**14,540**
At 31 December 2009							
Non-derivatives							
Trade payables	1,700	–	–	–	–	1,700	1,700
Borrowings (excluding finance leases)	1,439	1,439	910	2,595	6,321	12,704	11,869
Finance lease liabilities	61	61	120	355	149	746	575
Total non-derivatives	**3,200**	**1,500**	**1,030**	**2,950**	**6,470**	**15,150**	**14,144**

(All amounts in C thousands unless otherwise stated)

Financing arrangements

The Group's undrawn borrowing facilities were as follows as at 30 June 2010:

	30 June 2010	31 December 2009
Floating rate		
– Expiring within one year (bank overdraft and bill facility)	**7,400**	7,400
– Expiring beyond one year (bank loans)	**6,160**	4,470
	13,560	11,870

9 Equity securities issued

		Half-year			
		2010 Shares	2009 Shares	2010	2009
	Issues of ordinary shares during the half-year				
34p16(e)	Exercise of options issued under the VALUE ACCOUNTS Employee Option Plan	**45,600**	–	**104**	–
	Issued for no consideration:				
34p16(e)	Dividend reinvestment plan issues	**64,152**	58,983	**205**	174
		109,752	58,983	**309**	174
	Movements in treasury shares during the half-year				
34p16(e)	Acquisition of shares by the VALUE ACCOUNTS Employee Share Trust	**(145,000)**	(150,000)	**(459)**	(450)
34p16(e)	Employee share scheme issue	**143,290**	145,902	**454**	438
	Net movement	**(1,710)**	(4,098)	**(5)**	(12)

10 Dividends

		Half-year	
		2010	2009
	Ordinary shares		
34p16(f)	Dividends provided for or paid during the half-year	**989**	586
	6% cumulative redeemable preference shares		
	Dividends on these shares of C30,000 (2009: C30,000) have been recognised in the balance sheet as payables and have been charged to profit or loss as interest and finance charges because the shares are classified as liabilities	**432**	574

Dividends not recognised at the end of the half-year

In addition, an interim dividend of 5 cents per share (2009: 5 cents per share) was proposed by the board of directors on 20 July 2010 and approved by shareholders on 1 August 2010. It is payable on 31 October 2010 to shareholders who are on the register at 30 September 2010. This interim dividend, amounting to C432 (2009: C574), has not been recognised as a liability in these interim financial statements. It will be recognised in shareholders' equity in the year to 31 December 2010.

(All amounts in C thousands unless otherwise stated)

DV

11 Discontinued operations

(a) Description

34p16(c)(i) On 24 October 2008, the Group announced its intention to sell the machinery-hire division and initiated an active programme to locate a buyer and complete the sale. The division was sold on 27 February 2009 with effect from 1 March 2009. The division disposed of was reported in the financial statements for the half-year ending 30 June 2009 as a discontinued operation.

Financial information relating to the discontinued operation for the period to the date of disposal is set out below.

(b) Financial performance and cash flow information

The financial performance and cash flow information presented are for the two months ended 27 February 2009.

	Half-year	
	2010	2009
Revenue	–	1,200
Expenses	–	(1,109)
Profit before income tax	–	91
Income tax expense	–	(27)
Profit after income tax of discontinued operations	–	64
Gain on sale of the division before income tax	–	930
Income tax expense	–	(279)
Gain on sale of the division after income tax	–	651
Profit from discontinued operation	–	715
Net cash inflow from ordinary activities	–	1,166
Net cash inflow (outflow) from investing activities (2009 includes an inflow of C3,960,000 from the sale of the division)	–	3,960
Net cash (outflow) from financing activities	–	–
Net increase in cash generated by the division	–	5,126

IFRS 5p38
7p40(d)

(c) Carrying amounts of assets and liabilities

The carrying amounts of assets and liabilities as at 27 February 2009 were:

	27 February 2009
Property, plant and equipment	1,660
Trade receivables	1,200
Inventories	950
Total assets	3,810
Trade creditors	(390)
Provision for employee benefits	(40)
Total liabilities	(430)
Net assets	3,380

(All amounts in C thousands unless otherwise stated)

(d) Details of the sale of the division

	Half-year	
	2010	2009
Consideration received or receivable:		
Cash	–	3,960
Fair value of contingent consideration	–	100
Present value of amount due on 30 September 2012	–	250
Total disposal consideration	–	4,310
Carrying amount of net assets sold	–	(3,380)
Gain on sale before income tax	–	930
Income tax expense	–	(279)
Gain on sale after income tax	–	651

In the event that the operations of the machinery hire division achieve certain performance criteria during the period 1 March 2009 to 30 September 2011, as specified in an 'earn-out' clause in the sale agreement, additional cash consideration of up to C400,000 will be receivable. At the time of the sale, the fair value of the consideration was determined to be C100,000 and was recognised as an available-for-sale financial asset. As at 30 June 2010, the fair value was estimated to be C105,000.

34p16(i)

12 Business combinations

Current period

IFRS 3 (revised) was applied to the acquisition of Office Furnishings Company A on 1 March 2010. Contingent consideration of C50, 000 has been recognised at fair value at 1 March 2010. The contingent consideration would not have previously been recorded at the date of acquisition, as the payment to the former owners of Office Furnishings Company A of 10% of the profit of Office Furnishings Company A in excess of C500,000 for 2011 (up to a maximum undiscounted amount of C300,000) was not probable. Acquisition-related costs of C75, 000 have been recognised in the income statement. These would previously have been included in the consideration for the business combination.

IFRS3B64 (a-d) On 1 March 2010, VALUE ACCOUNTS Holdings acquired 93.8% of the issued shares in Office Furnishings Company A, a manufacturer of office furniture and equipment, for consideration of C3,800,000. The acquisition is expected to increase the group's market share and reduce cost through economies of scale.

Details of the purchase consideration, the net assets acquired and goodwill are as follows:

IFRS3B64(f)

Purchase consideration	
– Cash paid	3,750
– Contingent consideration	50
Total purchase consideration	**3,800**

(All amounts in C thousands unless otherwise stated)

IFRS3B64(i) The assets and liabilities recognised as a result of the acquisition are as follows:

	Fair value
Cash and cash equivalents	175
Property, plant and equipment	2,095
Customer list	285
Customer contracts	180
Inventories	1,010
Receivables	685
Payables	(380)
Employee benefit liabilities	(230)
Borrowings	(250)
Net deferred tax assets	120
Net identifiable assets acquired	3,690
Non-controlling interest	(250)
Goodwill	360
	3,800

IFRS3B64 (e),(k) The goodwill is attributable to Office Furnishings Company A's strong position and profitability in trading in the office furniture and equipment market, and synergies expected to arise after the company's acquisition of the new subsidiary. None of the goodwill is expected to be deductible for tax purposes.

(a) Acquisition-related costs

IFRS3 B64(m) Acquisition-related costs of C75,000 are included in the income statement.

(b) Contingent consideration

IFRS3 B64(g) The contingent consideration arrangement requires the Group to pay the former owners of Office Furnishings Company A 5% of the profit of Office Furnishings Company A, in excess of C500,000 for the year ending 31 December 2010, up to a maximum undiscounted amount of C300,000.

The potential undiscounted amount of all future payments that the Group could be required to make under this arrangement is between C nil and C300,000. The fair value of the contingent consideration arrangement of C50,000 was estimated by applying the income approach. The fair value estimates are based on a discount rate of 8% and assumed probability-adjusted profit in Office Furnishings Company A of C1,400,000 to C1,800,000.

IFRS3 B67(b) As at 30 June 2010, there was an increase of C35,000 recognised in profit or loss for the contingent consideration arrangement, as the assumed probability-adjusted profit in Office Furnishings Company A was recalculated to be in the region of C2,200,000 to C2,500,000.

(c) Acquired receivables

IFRS3 B64(h) The fair value of trade and other receivables is C685,000 and includes trade receivables with a fair value of C623,000. The gross contractual amount for trade receivables due is C705,000, of which C82,000 is expected to be uncollectible.

(d) Non-controlling interest

IFRS3 B64(o) The Group has chosen to recognise the non-controlling interest at its fair value for this acquisition. The fair value of the non-controlling interest in Office Furnishings Company A, an unlisted company, was estimated by applying a market approach and an income approach. The fair value estimates are based on:

- an assumed discount rate of 8%;
- an assumed terminal value based on a range of terminal EBITDA multiples between three and five times;
- long-term sustainable growth rate of 2%;
- assumed financial multiples of companies deemed to be similar to Office Furnishings Company A; and
- assumed adjustments because of the lack of control or lack of marketability that market participants would consider when estimating the fair value of the non-controlling interest in Office Furniture Company A.

(e) Revenue and profit contribution

IFRS3 B64(q) The acquired business contributed revenues of C230, 000 and net profit of C75,000 to the Group for the period from 1 March 2010 to 30 June 2010. If the acquisition had occurred on 1 January 2010, consolidated revenue and consolidated profit for the half-year ended 30 June 2010 would have been C32,205,000 and C3,754,000 respectively.

Prior period

On 1 April 2009, the parent entity acquired 70% of the issued share capital of VALUE ACCOUNTS Electronics UK Ltd. Details of this business combination were disclosed in note 43 of the group's annual financial statements for the year ended 31 December 2009.

13 Contingencies

Contingent liabilities

34p16(j) A claim for unspecified damages was lodged during the period against the furniture division. The company has disclaimed liability and is defending the action. No provision in relation to the claim has been recognised in the financial statements, as legal advice indicates that it is unlikely that any significant liability will arise.

34p16(c), 17(f) The claim lodged against VALUE ACCOUNTS Electronics UK Ltd in December 2009 and disclosed in note 40 of the annual financial statements was settled through mediation. A payment of C25,000 was made to the claimant.

14 Related-party transactions

34(16)(i), p17(j) During the half-year ended 30 June 2010, VALUE ACCOUNTS Holdings entered into a contract with Construction Company B for the construction of the new production facilities for the electronic equipment division. Mr A L Cunningham is a director and shareholder of Construction Company B. The contract is a fixed price contract for the sum of C1,300,000. It is based on normal commercial terms and conditions.

15 Events occurring after the reporting period

34p16(h) On 1 August 2010, VALUE ACCOUNTS Holdings acquired all of the issued shares in Office Furniture C, a manufacturer and retailer of premium office furniture and equipment, for cash consideration of C4,500,000.

(All amounts in C thousands unless otherwise stated)

The provisionally determined fair value of the net identifiable assets of the company at the date of acquisition was C4,090,000; the purchased goodwill amounted to C410,000.

The financial effects of the above transaction have not been brought to account at 30 June 2010. The operating results and assets and liabilities of the company will be brought to account from 1 August 2010.

Statement of directors' responsibility

DTR 4.1.12R, DTR 4.2.10R, DTR 4.2.3R(3), DTR 4.2.4R, DTR 4.2.10R(1), (3)-(4)

The directors confirm that, to the best of their knowledge, these condensed consolidated interim financial statements have been prepared in accordance with IAS 34 as adopted by the European Union[3]. The interim management report includes a fair review of the information required by DTR 4.2.7R and DTR 4.2.8R, namely:

- an indication of important events that have occurred during the first six months of the financial year and their impact on the condensed set of financial statements , and a description of the principal risks and uncertainties for the remaining six months of the financial year; and
- material related-party transactions in the first six months of the financial year and any material changes in the related party transactions described in the last Annual Report.

DV

The directors of VALUE ACCOUNTS Holdings are listed in the VALUE ACCOUNTS Holdings Annual Report for 31 December 2009, with the exception of the following changes in the period: Mr H I Dive retired on 4 April 2009, and Mrs Pike was appointed on 4 April 2009. A list of current directors is maintained on the VALUE ACCOUNTS Holdings Group website: www.valueifrs.com.

DTR 4.2.11 By order of the Board[4]

DTR 4.2.10(2) [Signature]
[Name]

DTR 4.2.10(2) Chief Executive

DTR 4.2.10(2) [Signature]
[Name]

DTR 4.2.10(2) Finance Director
[Date]

[3] In accordance with 4.2.10(4), a person making a responsibility statement that the information gives a true and fair view of the assets, liabilities, financial position and profit of the group may satisfy this requirement by including a statement that the condensed set of financial statements has been prepared in accordance with (a) IAS 34; (b) for UK issuers not using IFRS, pronouncements on interim reporting issued by the Accounting Standards Board; or (c) for all other issuers not using IFRS, a national accounting standard relating to interim reporting, provided always that a person making such a statement has reasonable grounds to be satisfied that the condensed set of financial statements prepared in accordance with such a standard is not misleading.

[4] The name and function of any person who makes a responsibility statement must be explicitly stated in the responsibility statement. The UKLA, in the March 2008 edition of 'List!' confirmed that in most cases this is expected to be either the whole board of directors or one or more directors on behalf of the board. The UKLA does not expect this information to be cross-referenced to other documents.

Auditors' review report – ISRE (UK&I) 2410

DTR 4.2.9
ISRE
(UK&I) 2410

PricewaterhouseCoopers LLP
Address
Country
Telephone
Facsimile

Independent review report to VALUE ACCOUNTS Holdings

Introduction

We have been engaged by the company to review the consolidated interim financial information in the interim financial report for the half-year ended 30 June 2010, which comprises the consolidated income statement, the consolidated statement of comprehensive income, the consolidated balance sheet, the consolidated statement of changes in equity, the consolidated statement of cash flows and related notes.[1] We have read the other information contained in the interim financial report and considered whether it contains any apparent misstatements or material inconsistencies with the information in the consolidated interim financial information.

Directors' responsibilities

The interim financial report is the responsibility of, and has been approved by, the directors. The directors are responsible for preparing the interim financial report in accordance with the Disclosure and Transparency Rules of the United Kingdom's Financial Services Authority.

As disclosed in note 2, the annual financial statements of the group are prepared in accordance with IFRSs as adopted by the European Union. The consolidated interim financial information included in this interim financial report has been prepared in accordance with International Accounting Standard 34, 'Interim Financial Reporting', as adopted by the European Union.

Our responsibility

Our responsibility is to express to the company a conclusion on the consolidated interim financial information in the interim financial report based on our review. This report, including the conclusion, has been prepared for and only for the company for the purpose of the Disclosure and Transparency Rules of the Financial Services Authority and for no other purpose. We do not, in producing this report, accept or assume responsibility for any other purpose or to any other person to whom this report is shown or into whose hands it may come save where expressly agreed by our prior consent in writing.

Scope of review

We conducted our review in accordance with International Standard on Review Engagements (UK and Ireland) 2410, 'Review of Interim Financial Information Performed by the Independent Auditor of the Entity' issued by the Auditing Practices Board for use in the United Kingdom. A review of interim financial information consists of making enquiries, primarily of persons responsible for financial and accounting matters, and applying analytical and other review procedures. A review is substantially less in scope than an audit conducted in accordance with International Standards on Auditing (UK and Ireland) and consequently does not enable us to obtain assurance that we would become aware of all significant matters that might be identified in an audit. Accordingly, we do not express an audit opinion.

[1] Review reports of entities that do not publish their interim financial reports on a web site or publish them using 'PDF' format may continue to refer to the pages of the interim financial report.

Conclusion

Based on our review, nothing has come to our attention that causes us to believe that the consolidated interim financial information in the interim financial report for the half-year s ended 30 June 2010 is not prepared, in all material respects, in accordance with International Accounting Standard 34 as adopted by the European Union and the Disclosure and Transparency Rules of the United Kingdom's Financial Services Authority.

PricewaterhouseCoopers LLP
Chartered Accountants
[Location]
[Date]

Notes:

(a) The maintenance and integrity of the VALUE ACCOUNTS Holdings web site is the responsibility of the directors; the work carried out by the auditors does not involve consideration of these matters and, accordingly, the auditors accept no responsibility for any changes that may have occurred to the interim financial report since it was initially presented on the web site.

(b) Legislation in the United Kingdom governing the preparation and dissemination of financial information may differ from legislation in other jurisdictions.

Appendix I – Alternative presentation of income statement – by nature of expense

		Notes	Half-year 2010	2009
34p20(b)				
	Revenue from continuing operations		**32,100**	26,174
	Other income		**485**	1,361
	Changes in inventories of finished goods and work in progress		**(136)**	250
	Raw materials and consumables used		**(10,870)**	(9,460)
	Employee benefits expense		**(13,632)**	(11,820)
	Depreciation and amortisation expense		**(833)**	(697)
	Impairment of goodwill		–	(410)
	Write off of assets damaged by fire		–	(1,210)
	Other expenses		**(2,307)**	(673)
	Finance costs		**(787)**	(608)
	Share of post-tax profits of associates and joint venture		**205**	340
	Profit before income tax		**4,225**	3,247
	Income tax expense		**(1,175)**	(909)
	Profit from continuing operations		**3,050**	2,338
	Profit from discontinued operation		–	715
	Profit for the half-year		**3,050**	3,053
	Profit is attributable to:			
	Owners of VALUE ACCOUNTS Holdings		**2,600**	2,565
	Non-controlling interests		**450**	488
			3,050	3,053
			Cents per share	Cents per share
34p11	**Earnings per share for profit from continuing operations attributable to the ordinary equity holders of the company:**			
	Basic earnings per share		**18.8**	15.9
	Diluted earnings per share		**18.0**	15.5
34p11	**Earnings per share for profit attributable to the ordinary equity holders of the company:**			
	Basic earnings per share		**18.8**	22.0
	Diluted earnings per share		**18.0**	21.5

The above consolidated income statement should be read in conjunction with the accompanying notes.

Appendix II – Alternative presentation of consolidated statement of cash flows – direct method

			Half-year	
34p8(d), 10, 20(d)		**Notes**	**2010**	2009
	Cash flows from operating activities			
	Receipts from customers		**33,070**	24,006
	Payments to suppliers and employees		**(24,426)**	(23,597)
			8,644	409
	Payments for financial assets at fair value through profit or loss		**(500)**	–
	Proceeds from disposal of financial assets at fair value through profit or loss		**650**	–
	Insurance recovery relating to fire	5	**–**	300
	Transaction costs relating to acquisition of subsidiary	12	**(75)**	(100)
	Other revenue		**180**	145
	Interest paid		**(893)**	(603)
	Income taxes paid		**(2,937)**	(1,147)
	Net cash inflow (outflow) from operating activities		**5,069**	(996)
	Cash flows from investing activities:			
	– acquisition of subsidiary, net of cash acquired	12	**(3,575)**	(1,500)
	– property, plant and equipment	6	**(2,060)**	(2,511)
	– investment property		**–**	(150)
	– available-for-sale financial assets		**(73)**	(27)
	– held-to-maturity investments		**(87)**	(150)
	– patents and trademarks		**(20)**	(9)
	– development costs		**(25)**	(58)
	– sale of machinery hire division	11	**–**	3,960
	– sale of property, plant and equipment		**2,425**	1,495
	– sale of available-for-sale financial assets		**49**	85
	Joint venture partnership distributions received		**250**	120
	Dividends received		**160**	150
	Interest received		**170**	180
	Net cash (outflow) inflow from investing activities		**(2,782)**	1,555
	Cash flows from financing activities:			
34p16(e)	– issues of shares and other equity securities	9	**104**	–
34p16(e)	– borrowings	8	**6,487**	4,500
	– shares acquired by the VALUE ACCOUNTS Employee Share Trust	9	**(460)**	(450)
34p16(e)	Repayment of borrowings		**(6,050)**	(3,400)
34p16(e)	Finance lease payments		**(15)**	(25)
34p16(f)	Dividends paid to company's shareholders		**(784)**	(412)
	Dividends paid to non-controlling interests in subsidiaries		**(185)**	(110)
	Net cash inflow (outflow) from financing activities		**(903)**	103
	Net increase (decrease) in cash and cash equivalents		**1,384**	662
	Cash and cash equivalents at the beginning of the half-year		**5,879**	562
	Effects of exchange rate changes on cash and cash equivalents		**5**	(7)
	Cash and cash equivalents at end of the half-year		**7,268**	1,217

The above consolidated statement of cash flows should be read in conjunction with the accompanying notes.

Appendix III – Example disclosures for first-time adopters

This appendix is an extract from PricewaterhouseCoopers' publication *Transitioning from Canadian GAAP in First-Time IFRS Interim Financial Statements – An Illustration.*

PwC observation. IFRS 1.23 requires companies to explain how the transition from previous Canadian GAAP to IFRS affected its financial position, performance and cash flows. To comply with this requirement, an entity must disclose reconciliations of its equity as previously reported under Canadian GAAP to IFRS as at (a) the date of the transition to IFRS, (b) the preceding annual year-end, and (c) the end of the comparative interim period. The entity must also disclose reconciliations of comprehensive income for the preceding annual year and the comparative interim period (IFRS 1.24). Reconciliations for annual periods can be excluded from an entity's first-time interim IFRS financial statements if the reconciliations are included in another published document and the interim financial statements include a cross-reference to that document (IFRS 1.32(b)).

IFRS 1 does not prescribe a particular method of presentation for reconciliations, except that the starting point for the reconciliation of comprehensive income shall be the total of comprehensive income in accordance with Canadian GAAP for the same period. Canadian securities regulators to date also have not established more specific requirements for reconciliations. These illustrative financial statements present two basic reconciliation formats. One format, illustrated in note 1(iii), reconciles total equity and total comprehensive income reported under Canadian GAAP to the totals reported under IFRS. This format is similar to the approach often used by Canadian companies that reconcile Canadian GAAP to US GAAP in SEC filings. The second format, illustrated in note 1(iii), provides a line by line reconciliation of items presented on the statements of financial position and comprehensive income. This approach is suggested in Example 11 of the IASB's implementation guidance to IFRS 1. In both cases it is necessary to provide explanatory notes for individual reconciling items, also illustrated below. Other formats are also possible.

IFRS 1 specifies that reconciliations must provide sufficient detail to enable users to understand the material adjustments to the statements of financial position and comprehensive income. Entities should carefully consider whether this condition has been met. This determination is a question of professional judgment and depends on the individual facts and circumstances. Factors that may be relevant to the determination include the nature, volume and complexity of material adjustments.

The question arises whether reconciliations also must include material adjustments other than those that affect equity or comprehensive income (e.g., balance sheet reclassifications affecting assets and liabilities, but not equity). The basis for conclusions to IFRS 1 states:

> Paragraphs 24(a) and (b) of the IFRS requires reconciliations of total equity and total comprehensive income. The Board concluded that users would also find it helpful to have information about the other adjustments that affect the opening IFRS balance sheet but do not appear in these reconciliations. Because a reconciliation could be voluminous, the IFRS requires disclosure of narrative information about these adjustments, as well as other about adjustments to the cash flow statements (paragraph 25 of the IFRS). (IFRS 1, BC92)

The reconciliation in note 1(iii), and the discussion of reconciling items, includes reclassification adjustments as well as adjustments that affect equity and comprehensive income.

IAS 34.16 requires an entity to discuss the nature and effect of significant changes to accounting policies arising in the period, if material. Providing this information as part of the notes to the reconciliation and explaining individual reconciling items, as illustrated below, is one way of meeting this requirement.

(All amounts in millions of Canadian dollars)

Sample Co.

Notes to Consolidated Interim Financial Statements
For the three months ended March 31, 2011 and 2010
(Unaudited)

1 Transition to IFRS

The effect of the company's transition to IFRS is summarized in this note as follows:

(i) Transition elections

(ii) Reconciliation of equity and comprehensive income as previously reported under Canadian GAAP to IFRS

(iii) Reconciliation of equity and comprehensive income as previously reported under Canadian GAAP to IFRS (alternative format)

(iv) Adjustments to the statement of cash flows

(i) Transition elections

The company has applied the following transition exceptions and exemptions to full retrospective application of IFRS:

	As described in note 1(iii)
Deemed cost of property, plant and equipment	(b)
Employee benefits – treatment of actuarial gains and losses	(g)
Cumulative translation adjustment	(n)
Business combinations	(p)
Hedge accounting	(q)

PwC observation. IFRS 1 does not explicitly require a summary of the transition exemptions and elections that an entity applies, but providing this information is common. It is a question of preference whether a discussion of the nature and effect of these exemptions and exceptions is included here or, as illustrated below, as part of the reconciliations of equity and comprehensive income.

(All amounts in millions of Canadian dollars)

(ii) Reconciliation of equity and comprehensive income as previously reported under Canadian GAAP to IFRS

		Dec 31, 2010	Mar 31, 2010	Jan 1, 2010
Equity	1(iii)	**$**	**$**	**$**
Equity as reported under Canadian GAAP		1,439	1,219	1,206
IFRS adjustments increase (decrease):				
Securitizations of trade receivables	**a**	2	3	2
Property, plant and equipment:				
– Revaluation	**b**	109	122	125
– Impairment	**c**	(23)	–	–
		86	122	125
Revaluation of available-for-sale equity investments	**d**	12	9	15
Share of IFRS adjustments relating to associate	**e**	25	26	27
Restructuring liability	**f**	(30)	–	–
Employee future benefits – actuarial gains and losses	**g**	(14)	(19)	(19)
Employee future benefits – past service costs	**h**	(19)	(21)	(23)
		(33)	(40)	(42)
Deferred income tax	**i**	(14)	(33)	(33)
Warrants	**j**	(81)	(74)	(72)
Non-controlling interests	**k**	252	250	243
Equity as reported under IFRS		1,658	1,482	1,471

(All amounts in millions of Canadian dollars)

Comprehensive income	**1(iii)**	**Year ended Dec 31, 2010 $**	**Three months ended Mar 31, 2010 $**
As reported under Canadian GAAP		208	5
Increase (decrease) in net income for:			
Adjustment on securitization of receivables	**a**	–	1
Depreciation on revaluation of property, plant and equipment	**b**	(16)	(3)
Impairment of property, plant and equipment	**c**	(23)	–
Share of IFRS adjustments relating to associate	**e**	(2)	(1)
Restructuring expenses	**f**	(30)	–
Employee future benefits – past service costs	**h**	4	2
Deferred income tax	**i**	32	(1)
Fair value adjustment on warrants	**j**	(9)	(2)
Non-controlling interest	**k**	9	7
Share-based payments amortization	**l**	2	1
Impairment of debt securities	**o**	(44)	–
Change in fair value of cash flow hedges	**q**	6	3
		(71)	7
Increase (decrease) in other comprehensive income for:			
Change in fair value of equity investments	**d**	(3)	(6)
Employee future benefits – actuarial gains and losses	**g**	5	–
Deferred income tax	**i**	(13)	1
Impairment of debt securities	**o**	44	–
Change in fair value of cash flow hedges	**q**	(6)	(3)
		27	(8)
As reported under IFRS		164	4

PwC observation. Sample Co. has elected to provide separate reconciliations of net income and other comprehensive income within its overall reconciliation of comprehensive income. IFRS 1 does not specifically require this distinction to be made. It does, however, assist readers in understanding the financial statements.

(All amounts in millions of Canadian dollars)

(iii) Reconciliation of equity and comprehensive income as previously reported under Canadian GAAP to IFRS (alternative format)

		December 31, 2010			March 31, 2010			January 1, 2010		
	1(iii)	Cdn GAAP	Adj	IFRS	Cdn GAAP	Adj	IFRS	Cdn GAAP	Adj	IFRS
Assets										
Current assets										
Cash and cash equivalents		251	–	251	46	–	46	136	–	136
Marketable securities		144	–	144	107	–	107	151	–	151
Trade receivables	a	193	103	296	142	107	249	195	100	295
Inventories		331	–	331	623	–	623	402	–	402
Other current assets	a	67	(5)	62	66	(6)	60	63	(5)	58
		986	98	1,084	984	101	1,085	947	95	1,042
Non-current assets										
Debt and equity securities	d, o	101	12	113	145	9	154	147	15	162
Property, plant and equipment	b, c	1,246	86	1,332	1,292	122	1,414	1,232	125	1,357
Investments in associates	e	370	25	395	317	26	343	306	27	333
Intangible assets		141	–	141	101	–	101	108	–	108
Goodwill		217	–	217	217	–	217	217	–	217
		3,061	221	3,282	3,056	258	3,314	2,957	262	3,219
Liabilities										
Current liabilities										
Trade payables		122	–	122	131	–	131	108	–	108
Short-term debt	a	302	96	398	520	98	618	329	93	422
Current portion of long-term debt		115	–	115	120	–	120	123	–	123
Income tax liabilities		53	–	53	9	–	9	49	–	49
Warrants	j	–	81	81	–	74	74	–	72	72
Other derivative liabilities	q	12	–	12	9	–	9	6	–	6
Deferred income tax liabilities	i	10	(10)	–	10	(10)	–	11	(11)	-
Other liabilities	f	24	30	54	66	–	66	147	–	147
		638	197	835	865	162	1,027	773	154	927
Non-current liabilities										
Long-term debt		238	–	238	293	–	293	303	–	303
Deferred income tax liabilities	i, m	165	24	189	106	43	149	94	44	138
Post-employment benefit obligations	g, h	329	33	362	323	40	363	338	42	380
		1,370	254	1,624	1,587	245	1,832	1,508	240	1,748
Non-controlling interests	k	**252**	**(252)**	–	**250**	**(250)**	–	**243**	**(243)**	–
Equity										
Share capital		250	–	250	250	–	250	250	–	250
Contributed surplus	l	107	3	110	90	4	94	82	5	87
Warrants	j	50	(50)	–	50	(50)	–	50	(50)	–
Accumulated other comprehensive income	r	(55)	41	(14)	(37)	6	(31)	(31)	14	(17)
Retained earnings	s	1,087	(37)	1,050	866	42	908	855	41	896
Non-controlling interest	k	–	262	262	–	261	261	–	255	255
		1,439	219	1,658	1,219	263	1,482	1,206	265	1,471
		3,061	221	3,282	3,056	258	3,314	2,957	262	3,219

(All amounts in millions of Canadian dollars)

		Year ended December 31, 2010			Three months ended March 31, 2010		
	1(iii)	Cdn GAAP	Adj	IFRS	Cdn GAAP	Adj	IFRS
Revenues		2,153	–	2,153	278	–	278
Cost of sales	b, h, c	1,670	35	1,705	216	5	221
Gross profit		483	(35)	448	62	(5)	57
General and administration	f, l	(132)	(28)	(160)	(25)	1	(24)
Sales and marketing		(107)	–	(107)	(14)	–	(14)
Research and development		(18)	–	(18)	(4)	–	(4)
Other gains and losses (net)	a, j, o	94	(23)	71	6	6	12
Share of income of associates	e	64	(2)	62	11	(1)	10
		384	(88)	296	36	1	37
Interest income		17	–	17	3	–	3
Interest expense	a, q	(46)	(24)	(70)	(11)	(4)	(15)
Net interest expense		(29)	(24)	(53)	(8)	(4)	(12)
Income before income tax		355	(112)	243	28	(3)	25
Non-controlling interest	k	(9)	9	–	(7)	7	-
Income tax	i	(114)	32	(82)	(10)	3	(7)
Net income (loss) for the period		232	(71)	161	11	7	18
Attributable to:							
Owners of the parent				154			12
Non-controlling interests				7			6
Other comprehensive income (net of tax):							
Cumulative translation adjustment		29	–	29	(5)	–	(5)
Changes in fair value of available-for-sale investments	d	(46)	28	(18)	(2)	(5)	(7)
Changes in the fair value of cash flow hedges	q	5	(4)	1	3	(3)	-
Share of other comprehensive income of associates		(12)	–	(12)	(2)	–	(2)
Actuarial gain (loss) on post-employment benefit obligations	g	–	3	3	–	–	-
Other comprehensive income (loss) for the period		(24)	27	3	(6)	(8)	(14)
Comprehensive income (loss)		208	(44)	164	5	(1)	4

Explanatory notes

PwC observation. The following explanatory notes describe:

- Material adjustments to the statements of financial position and comprehensive income arising from the adoption of IFRS;
- Significant differences between Canadian GAAP and IFRS applicable to Sample Co.; and
- The transition elections and exemptions Sample Co. applied in preparing its opening IFRS balance sheet.

How much detail to provide in explanatory notes is a question of judgment that will depend, in part, on the reconciliation approach that an entity uses. As explained earlier, the reconciliation, in combination with the explanatory notes, should be sufficient to enable users to understand the material adjustments to the statements of financial position and statements of comprehensive income, including material adjustments that did not affect equity or comprehensive income. In some cases, the reconciliation format in 1(iii) may provide the most effective way of communicating the required information.

The explanatory notes discuss the effect of individual adjustments on individual line items on the statements of financial position and comprehensive income. This disclosure would not be required if it is already apparent from the reconciliations themselves.

(a) Securitizations of trade receivables that were accounted for as sales under Canadian GAAP have been accounted for as collateralized borrowings under IFRS. Under IFRS, the company accounts for transfers of trade receivables as sales only if substantially all of the risks and rewards of ownership are transferred. If not, the transfer is treated as a financing. Under Canadian GAAP, sales were recognized when the company transferred control of the receivables. At January 1, 2010, this adjustment increased trade receivables and short-term debt by $100 and $93 ($107 and $98 at March 31, 2010, and $103 and $96 at December 31, 2010) and eliminated the company's retained interest in transferred receivables of $5, included in other assets ($6 at March 31, 2010 and $5 at December 31, 2010). Losses on transfers, included in other gains and losses (net) on the statement of income under Canadian GAAP of $5 for the three months ended March 31, 2010 and $24 for the year ended December 31, 2010 have been eliminated and interest expense on the borrowings of $4 at March 31, 2010 and $24 at December 31, 2010 has been recognized under IFRS.

(b) In accordance with IFRS transitional provisions, the company elected to revalue by $125 certain property, plant and equipment to its fair value of $857 at January 1, 2010. The resulting increased depreciation expense of $3 for the three months ended March 31, 2010 and $16 for the year ended December 31, 2010 was included in cost of sales. Adjustments to the consolidated statement of financial position at March 31, 2010 and December 31, 2010 of $122 and $109 are net of accumulated depreciation.

PwC observation. If an entity elects on transition to use fair value as deemed cost for an item of property, plant and equipment, an investment property or an intangible asset, IFRS 1.30 requires it to disclose, for each line item in the opening IFRS statement of financial position, the aggregate of those fair values and the aggregate adjustment to the carrying amounts reported under Canadian GAAP.

(All amounts in millions of Canadian dollars)

(c) An impairment loss of $23 relating to property, plant and equipment was recognized in cost of sales at December 31, 2010 for property, plant and equipment for which an impairment indicator existed at December 31, 2010 (see note 2). This impairment was not recognized under Canadian GAAP. This adjustment arose because under IFRS the recoverable amount used in recognizing and measuring an impairment is the higher of the asset's fair value less costs to sell and its value in use. Under Canadian GAAP, the recoverable amount used to determine whether recognition of an impairment loss is required is the undiscounted future cash flows expected from its use and eventual disposition.

(d) Under IFRS, available-for-sale equity investments not quoted in an active market must be measured at fair value, unless fair value cannot be reliably measured. Under Canadian GAAP, such assets were measured at cost. The adjustments to the carrying value of the investment to recognize this difference were $15 at January 1, 2010, $9 at March 31, 2010 and $12 at December 31, 2010. Declines in fair value from January 1, 2010 of $6 for the three months ended March 31, 2010 and $3 for the year ended December 31, 2010 are recognized in other comprehensive income until the investment is sold or written down as impaired.

(e) The adjustment to the investment in associate of $27 at January 1, 2010 ($26 at March 31, 2011 and $25 at December 31, 2011) recognizes the company's share of the investee's adjustments arising from its transition from Canadian GAAP to IFRS (relating primarily to the investee's election to revalue property, plant and equipment at the date of transition to IFRS). The company's share of the resulting increase in depreciation expense, net of applicable income tax, of $1 for the three months ended March 31, 2010 and $2 for the year ended December 31, 2010 has been included in the company's share of income of associates. Adjustments to the consolidated statement of financial position at March 31, 2010 and December 31, 2010 are net of accumulated depreciation.

(f) On December 30, 2010, the company announced its decision to streamline certain head office functions and eliminate certain management positions. The company offered severance packages to certain employees which they may voluntarily accept prior to January 28, 2011. In accordance with IFRS, restructuring charges of $30 related to termination benefits for employees expected to accept the offer have been accrued at December 31, 2010. Restructuring costs are included within general and administrative expenses. Under Canadian GAAP, termination benefits for voluntary terminations are accrued only when employees accept the offer. No offers had been accepted at December 31, 2010 and consequently no restructuring costs were recognized.

(g) Under IFRS, the company recognizes actuarial gains and losses arising from the re-measurement of employee future benefit obligations in other comprehensive income as they arise. Under Canadian GAAP, the company applied the corridor method of accounting for such gains and losses. Under this method, gains and losses are recognized only if they exceed specified thresholds. The carrying value of the net liability for employee future benefit obligations has been increased by $19 to recognize cumulative net actuarial gains and losses accumulated as at January 1, 2010, which was reduced to $14 at December 31, 2010 to recognize the actuarial gain of $5 for the year ($3 net of income tax). No actuarial gains and losses were recognized under Canadian GAAP using the corridor approach.

(h) Under IFRS, the company expenses the cost of past service benefits awarded to employees under post-employment benefit plans over the periods in which the benefits vest, which usually corresponds to the period in which the benefits are granted. Under Canadian GAAP, the company expensed past service costs over the weighted average service life of active employees remaining in the plan. This adjustment increased the net liability for employee future benefits in the statement of financial position by $23 at January 1, 2010, $21 at March 31, 2010 and $19 at December 31, 2010 and reduced cost of sales by $2 and $4 for the three months ended March 31, 2010 and year ended December 31, 2010 respectively.

(All amounts in millions of Canadian dollars)

(i) Deferred income tax liabilities have been adjusted to give effect to adjustments as follows:

	Ref	Dec 31, 2010	Mar 31, 2010	Jan 1, 2010
Property, plant and equipment:				
– Revaluation	b	36	40	41
– Impairment	c	(8)	–	-
Revaluation of available-for-sale equity investments	d	2	1	2
Share of IFRS adjustments relating to associate	e	4	4	4
Restructuring liability	f	(10)	–	-
Employee future benefits – actuarial gains and losses	g	(4)	(6)	(6)
Employee future benefits – past service costs	h	(6)	(6)	(8)
		14	33	33

The above adjustments increased (decreased) deferred income tax expense recognized in the income statement by $1 for the three months ended March 31, 2010 and ($32) for the year ended December 31, 2010, The adjustments increased (decreased) deferred income tax expense recognized in other comprehensive income by ($1) for the three months ended March 31, 2011 and $13 for the year ended December 31, 2010.

(j) The warrants entitle the holder to acquire a fixed number of common shares for a fixed US dollar price per share. In accordance with IFRS, an obligation to issue shares for a price that is not fixed in the company's functional currency, and that does not qualify as a rights offering, must be classified as a derivative liability and measured at fair value with changes recognized in the statement of income as they arise. The company has recorded these changes in other gains and losses. Under Canadian GAAP, the warrants were classified as equity and changes in fair value were not recognized. This change in accounting increased liabilities at January 1, 2010 by $72 ($74 at March 31, 2010 and $81 at December 31, 2010) and reduced other gains and losses by $2 and $9 for the three months ended March 31, 2010 and the year ended December 31, 2010, respectively.

(k) Under IFRS, the non-controlling interests' share of the net assets of subsidiaries is included in equity and their share of the comprehensive income of subsidiaries is allocated directly to equity. Under Canadian GAAP, non-controlling interests were presented as a separate item between liabilities and equity in the statement of financial position and the non-controlling interests' share of income and other comprehensive income were deducted in calculating net income and comprehensive income of the entity. Non-controlling interest of $243 at January 1, 2010 ($250 at March 31, 2010 and $252 at December 31, 2010) as determined under Canadian GAAP has been reclassified to equity.

The non-controlling interests' cumulative share of adjustments recognized on the adoption of IFRS was $12 at January 1, 2010, $11 at March 31, 2010 and $10 at December 31, 2010. The non-controlling interests' share of net income of $7 for the three months ended March 31, 2010 and $9 for the year ended December 31, 2010 has been eliminated in the statement of income.

(l) Under IFRS the company accrues the cost of employee stock options over the vesting period using the graded method of amortization rather than the straight-line method, which was the company's policy under Canadian GAAP. This increased contributed surplus and reduced retained earnings at the date of transition and increased general and administration expenses by $1 for the three months ended March 31, 2010 and $2 for the year ended December 31, 2010.

(m) Under IFRS, it is not appropriate to classify deferred income tax balances as current, irrespective of the classification of the assets or liabilities to which the deferred income tax relates or the expected timing of reversal. Under Canadian GAAP, deferred income tax relating to current assets or current liabilities must be classified as current. Accordingly, current

(All amounts in millions of Canadian dollars)

deferred income tax reported under Canadian GAAP of $11 at January 1, 2010 ($10 at March 31, 2010 and December 31, 2010) has been reclassified as non-current under IFRS.

(n) In accordance with IFRS transitional provisions, the company has elected to reset the cumulative translation adjustment account, which includes gains and losses arising from the translation of foreign operations, to zero at the date of transition to IFRS. Accumulated other comprehensive income has been increased and retained earnings has been reduced by $14.

(o) The company recognized an impairment loss of $44 on available-for-sale debt securities under IFRS but not Canadian GAAP at December 31, 2010. Under IFRS, an impairment loss must be recognized for an investment in an available-for-sale debt security if there is objective evidence of impairment. Under Canadian GAAP, impairment losses are not recognized unless a decline in fair value occurred that is other than temporary. This adjustment reduced retained earnings and increased accumulated other comprehensive income at December 31, 2010 by the same amount.

(p) In accordance with IFRS transitional provisions, the company elected to apply IFRS relating to business combinations prospectively from January 1, 2010. As such, Canadian GAAP balances relating to business combinations entered into before that date, including goodwill, have been carried forward without adjustment.

(q) The company held interest rate swaps at the transition date as hedges of cash flow risk related to the company's variable rate debt instruments. Under Canadian GAAP, the swaps were accounted for as hedges. Changes in their fair value were initially recognized in other comprehensive income and transferred to the statement of income as the variable interest expense was recognized on the debt instrument. The method of assessing hedge effectiveness used under Canadian GAAP did not qualify these instruments for hedge accounting under IFRS and the company has discontinued hedge accounting prospectively on transition to IFRS. As a result, changes in the fair value of the swap occurring after January 1, 2010 under IFRS are recognized directly in other gains and losses (net). This increased other gains by $3 for the three months ended March 31, 2010 and $6 for the year ended December 31, 2010. In accordance with IFRS transition requirements, gains and losses on the swaps arising prior to January 1, 2010 continue to be recognized in accumulated other comprehensive income pending the occurrence of the hedged transactions.

(r) The following is a summary of transition adjustments to the company's accumulated other comprehensive income from Canadian GAAP to IFRS:

	Ref	Dec 31, 2010	Mar 31, 2010	Jan 1, 2010
Accumulated other comprehensive income as reported under Canadian GAAP		(55)	(37)	(31)
IFRS adjustments increase (decrease):				
Revaluation of available-for-sale equity investments	d	12	9	15
Employee future benefits – actuarial gains and losses	g	(14)	(19)	(19)
Deferred income tax	i	(9)	5	4
Cumulative translation adjustment	n	14	14	14
Impairment of debt securities	o	44	–	–
Cash flow hedges	q	(6)	(3)	–
		41	6	14
Accumulated other comprehensive income as reported under IFRS		(14)	(31)	(17)

(All amounts in millions of Canadian dollars)

(s) The following is a summary of transition adjustments to the company's retained earnings from Canadian GAAP to IFRS:

	Ref	Dec 31, 2010	Mar 31, 2010	Jan 1, 2010
Retained earnings as reported under Canadian GAAP		1,087	866	855
IFRS adjustments increase (decrease):				
Securitizations of trade receivables	a	2	3	2
Property, plant and equipment:				
– Revaluation	b	109	122	125
– Impairment	c	(23)	–	–
		86	122	125
Share of IFRS adjustments relating to associate	e	25	26	27
Restructuring liability	f	(30)	–	–
Impairment of debt securities	o	(44)	–	–
Employee future benefits – past service costs	h	(19)	(21)	(23)
Deferred income tax	i	(3)	(38)	(37)
Warrant liability	j	(31)	(24)	(22)
Non-controlling interest	k	(10)	(11)	(12)
Amortization of employee stock options	l	(3)	(4)	(5)
Cumulative translation adjustment	n	(14)	(14)	(14)
Cash flow hedges	r	4	3	-
		(37)	42	41
Retained earnings as reported under IFRS		1,050	908	896

(All amounts in millions of Canadian dollars)

(iv) Adjustments to the statement of cash flows

The transition from Canadian GAAP to IFRS had no significant impact on cash flows generated by the company except that, under IFRS, cash flows relating to interest are classified as operating, investing or financing in a consistent manner each period. Under Canadian GAAP, cash flows relating to interest payments were classified as operating.

2 Additional IFRS information for the year ended December 31, 2010

PwC observation. IFRS 1.33 states that if a first-time adopter did not, in its most recent annual financial statements in accordance with previous GAAP, disclose information material to an understanding of the current interim period, its interim financial report should disclose that information or include a cross-reference to another published document that includes that information. The basis for conclusions on IFRS 1 explains this requirement further, as follows:

> " ... an entity's interim financial report in accordance with IAS 34 is less helpful to users if the entity's latest annual financial statements were prepared using previous GAAP than if they were prepared in accordance with IFRS. Therefore, the Board concluded that a first-time adopter's first interim financial report in accordance with IAS 34 should include sufficient information to enable users to understand how the transition to IFRS affected previously reported annual, as well as interim figures ... (IFRS 1, BC96)."

The following items are examples of disclosures required in annual IFRS financial statements that were not disclosed previously under Canadian GAAP, or for which amounts have been significantly affected as a result of the transition to IFRS. We are providing this information solely to illustrate some of the types of disclosures that might be necessary should an entity conclude that the information is material. **It should not be inferred from these illustrations that such disclosures are always appropriate or that other disclosures are unnecessary.**

The following IFRS disclosures relating to the year ended December 31, 2010 are material to an understanding of these interim financial statements.

(i) Critical accounting estimates and judgments

The company makes estimates and assumptions concerning the future that will, by definition, seldom equal actual results. The following are estimates and judgments not previously made under Canadian GAAP that have a significant risk of causing a material adjustment to the carrying amounts of assets and liabilities within the next financial year.

(a) Critical accounting estimates

i. Fair value of property, plant and equipment

On January 1, 2010, the company increased the carrying value of certain of its property, plant and equipment to its fair value of $857(note 1(iii)(b)). The fair value of the property, plant and equipment was determined by recent market transactions for similar assets. Based on these transactions, management estimated that the range of reasonably possible values for the assets would be between $834 and $901.

ii. Estimated impairment of property, plant and equipment

An impairment charge of $23 arose in the manufacturing CGU "Factory A" which is the company's manufacturing plant in Ontario, Canada, following a decision in December 2010 to reduce the manufacturing output allocated to the operation. This was a result of the company's reallocation of manufacturing volumes due to decreasing demand in Factory A's region. The company reassessed the depreciation policies in the CGU and concluded that the useful life and residual values of property, plant and equipment will not be affected following this decision. The impairment charge is included in other gains and losses within the statement of income and in the segment reporting for Canada in note 9.

The recoverable amount of this CGU was estimated based on value-in-use calculations as this was determined to be higher than fair value less costs to sell. These calculations use cash flow projections based on financial budgets approved by management covering a five-year period. Cash flows beyond the five-year period are extrapolated using the estimated growth rates stated below. The growth rate does not exceed the long-term average growth rates for the manufacturing business in which the CGU operates. The following are key assumptions used in the value-in-use calculation:

Budgeted gross margin	27.5%
Weighted average growth rate used to extrapolate cash flows beyond the budget period	1.2%
Pre-tax discount rate applied in cash flow projections	10.5%

Management determined the budgeted gross margin based on past performance and its expectations for market development. The weighted average growth rates used are consistent with forecasts included in industry reports. The discount rates used are pre-tax and reflect specific risks in relation to the relevant CGU.

A change in management's gross margin estimate by 10% would increase the impairment by $2.5. If management reduces the growth rate by 10%, impairment would increase by $0.4. An increase in the discount rate by 10% would increase impairment by $1.8.

iii. Fair value of available-for-sale equity securities

The fair value of the company's available-for-sale equity securities that are not traded in an active market are determined using valuation techniques. The company has used an earnings approach to value these securities, based on earnings multiples for recent transactions involving similar businesses. If the applicable multiples were to increase or decrease by 0.5, the value of the securities would be an estimated $6 higher, or lower.

(All amounts in millions of Canadian dollars)

(b) Critical accounting judgments

i. Cash and cash equivalents

The company holds investments in highly liquid money market investment funds. The determination of whether a money market fund qualifies as a cash equivalent requires significant judgment. In determining whether such investments qualify as cash equivalents, the company considers the following criteria: whether all investments held by the fund qualify individually as cash equivalents, the fund's management and investment policies and any position papers issued by the associated financial institution or others.

(ii) Fair value of financial instruments

The following table summarizes the classification of the company's financial instruments that are measured at fair value under IFRS, which were previously measured on a different basis under Canadian GAAP:

	December 31, 2010			
	Level 1	**Level 2**	**Level 3**	**Total**
	$	**$**	**$**	**$**
Available-for-sale investments:				
Equity securities	–	–	59	59
	–	–	59	59
Derivative liabilities:				
Warrants	81	–	–	81
	81	–	–	81

The fair value of the company's available-for-sale equity securities has been measured using an earnings based valuation approach that assumes an EBITDA multiple of 4.5, which was estimated based on multiples for recent transactions involving similar companies.

PwC observation. Entities that have significant changes in the basis of measurement of financial assets and financial liabilities as the result of adopting IFRS should consider whether these changes would require the entity to update 2010 market risk and other financial instrument disclosures.

(All amounts in millions of Canadian dollars)

The following gains and losses have been included in net income for the year ended December 31, 2010, that were not previously included in net income under Canadian GAAP:

	Year ended December 31, 2010 $
Financial instruments held for trading:	
-- Fair value losses	(3)
– Fair value gains	6
Impairment loss on:	
-- Available-for-sale investments	(44)

(iii) Property, plant and equipment

Net book value	Year ended December 31, 2010			
	Land $	Buildings $	Plant and equipment $	Total $
At January 1, 2010:				
Cost	100	704	938	1,742
Accumulated depreciation	–	(172)	(213)	(385)
	100	532	725	1,357
At January 1, 2010:	100	532	725	1,357
Additions	–	–	104	104
Disposals	–	(33)	–	(33)
Depreciation for the year	–	(20)	(37)	(57)
Exchange differences	(2)	(6)	(8)	(16)
Impairment	–	–	(23)	(23)
At December 31, 2010	98	473	761	1,332
At December 31, 2010:				
Cost	98	663	1,008	1,769
Accumulated depreciation	–	(190)	(247)	(437)
	98	473	761	1,332

(All amounts in millions of Canadian dollars)

(iv) Intangible assets

Net book value	Year ended December 31, 2010 $
At January 1, 2010:	
Cost	137
Accumulated amortization	(29)
	108
At January 1, 2010:	108
Additions	45
Disposals	–
Amortization for the year	(11)
Exchange differences	(1)
Impairment	–
At December 31, 2010	141
At December 31, 2010:	
Cost	181
Accumulated amortization	(40)
	141

(v) Investments in associates

The following summarizes financial information about the company's share of assets, liabilities, revenue and profit or loss of its unlisted associate for the year ended December 31, 2010. The amounts disclosed include adjustments made to the carrying amount of the assets and liabilities of the associate on its acquisition and therefore may differ from the amounts recorded in the books and records of the associate.

	$
Assets	762
Liabilities	367
Revenues	725
Profit or loss	62

PwC observation. IAS 28, *Investments in Associates* ("IAS 28"), specifies annual disclosures related to investments in associates, including summarized financial information of associates for aggregated assets, liabilities, revenue, and profit or loss. IAS 28 does not specify whether this summarized financial information is the total amount of the associate's aggregated assets, liabilities, revenue and profit or loss that needs to be disclosed or the investor's share. IAS 28 also does not specify whether the disclosure should be based on IFRS book values in the financial statements of the associate or the IFRS carrying values notionally recognized by the investor as a result of the notional purchase price allocation. We believe either approach is acceptable but it must be consistently applied and explained clearly.

(All amounts in millions of Canadian dollars)

(vi) Other liabilities

	Restructuring $	Warranties $	Legal claims $	Total $
At January 1, 2010	–	42	105	147
Additional provisions	30	18	2	50
Unused amounts reversed	–	(2)	–	(2)
Utilized during the period	–	(31)	(107)	(138)
Exchange differences	–	(3)	–	(3)
At December 31, 2010	30	24	–	54

On December 30, 2010, the company announced its decision to streamline certain head office functions and eliminate redundancies in management and administrative positions. As part of this initiative, the company expects to incur one-time restructuring charges of $30 primarily related to termination benefits for employees expected to be paid out over the next fourteen months. Restructuring costs are included within general and administrative expenses in the consolidated statement of income.

(vii) Compensation of key management

Compensation awarded to key management included:

	Year ended December 31, 2010 $
Salaries and short-term employee benefits	62
Post-employment benefits	3
Share-based payments	9
Termination benefits	30
	104

(viii) Expense by nature

	Year ended December 31, 2010 $
Changes in inventories of finished goods and work in progress	71
Raw materials and consumables used	802
Depreciation, amortization and impairment charges	67
Employee benefits (ix)	598
Transportation	301
Advertising	14
Other expenses	28
	1,881

(All amounts in millions of Canadian dollars)

(ix) Employee benefits

	Year ended December 31, 2010 $
Salaries and wages	475
Pension costs – defined contribution plans	22
Pension costs – defined benefit plans	41
Stock-based compensation	23
Termination benefits – restructuring (note 6)	30
Other	7
	598

PwC observation. IAS 1.104 requires that an entity classifying expenses by function should disclose additional information on the nature of expenses, including depreciation and amortization expense and employee benefits expense. In this connection, employee benefits include all forms of consideration given by an entity in exchange for services rendered by employees. IAS 1.05 explains that an entity should select the presentation (i.e., function or nature) that is reliable and more relevant, taking into account historical and industry factors and the nature of the entity. However, because information on the nature of expenses is useful in predicting future cash flows, additional disclosure is necessary when the functional expense classification is used.

(x) Earnings per share

i. Basic

Basic earnings per share is calculated by dividing the net income attributable to owners of the parent by the weighted average number of ordinary shares in issue during the year.

	Year ended December 31, 2010
Net income attributable to owners of the parent	154
Weighted average number of ordinary shares in issue	257,131,000
Basic earnings per share	$0.60

(All amounts in millions of Canadian dollars)

ii. Diluted

Diluted earnings per share is calculated by adjusting the weighted average number of ordinary shares outstanding to assume conversion of all dilutive potential ordinary shares. The company has two categories of dilutive potential ordinary shares: warrants and stock options. For both, a calculation is done to determine the number of shares that could have been acquired at fair value (determined as the average market share price of the company's outstanding shares for the period) based on the monetary value of the subscription rights attached to the warrants and stock options. The number of shares calculated above is compared with the number of shares that would have been issued assuming the exercise of the warrants and stock options.

	Year ended December 31, 2010
Net income attributable to owners of the parent	154
Weighted average number of ordinary shares in issue	257,131,000
Adjustments for:	
Warrants	50,000,000
Stock options	7,261,353
Weighted average number of ordinary shares for diluted earnings per share	314,392,353
Diluted earnings per share	$0.49

(All amounts in millions of Canadian dollars)

3 Debt

PwC observation. This and the following notes are examples of notes describing significant events and transactions that are significant to an understanding of changes in Sample Co.'s financial position and performance since the end of the last reporting period. Disclosure of these events and transactions is required by IAS 34.16. IAS 34 also requires an entity to provide segment information in interim financial statements if IFRS 8, *Operating Segments*, requires this disclosure in annual financial statements and, if a business combination has occurred during the interim period, the disclosures required by IFRS 3, Business Combinations. Our publication *Illustrating Interim Financial Information for Existing IFRS Preparers* provides comprehensive examples of IAS 34 interim financial reporting requirements.

	March 31, 2011 $	December 31, 2010 $
Short-term debt:		
Opening balance at January 1	398	422
New debt	312	1,208
Repayment of debt	(616)	(1,232)
Closing balance	94	398
Long-term debt:		
Opening balance at January 1	353	426
New debt	550	242
Transaction costs	(19)	(7)
Repayment of debt	(353)	(308)
Closing balance	531	353
Current portion	–	115
Non-current portion	531	238
	531	353

On March 27, 2011, Sample Co. restructured its long-term debt by entering into a credit agreement with a Canadian chartered bank providing for a senior secured credit facility in the amount of $1,500 with a maturity date of July 27, 2013. Outstanding amounts drawn on the line of credit are collateralized by the assets of Sample Co. and its subsidiaries. Interest is based on prime plus a margin. At March 31, 2011, $550 was drawn on the facility at a blended interest rate of 3.83%. No gain or loss was recognized on the settlement of the company's previously outstanding debt as it was settled for an amount that approximated its amortized cost at the date of settlement.

(All amounts in millions of Canadian dollars)

4 Restructuring liability

Included in other liabilities are restructuring costs of $20 as at March 31, 2011 ($30 as at December 31, 2010). During the period, the company incurred an additional $5 million of restructuring expenses, included in general and administration expenses, and paid out $15 million to settle existing restructuring obligations.

PwC observation. IAS 1.97 states that when an item of income or expense is material, the nature and amount should be disclosed separately. Similarly, IAS 34.16(c) requires disclosure of the nature and amount of items affecting assets, liabilities, equity, net income, or cash flows that are unusual because of their nature, size, or incidence. Examples of such disclosures include write-downs of inventories, or property, plant and equipment, reversals of write-downs, restructurings of the activities of an entity and reversals of any provisions for the costs of restructuring, disposals of property, plant and equipment, disposals of investments, discontinued operations, litigations settlements and other reversals of provisions.

In accordance with its "by function" basis of expense classification, during the three months ended March 31, 2011, Sample Co. has included "unusual items" consisting of an additional restructuring charge of $5 million (described in the note above) and an impairment of an available-for-sale investment of $18 million (described in note 5 below) in general and administration expense and other gains and losses (net) (similar items relating to 2010 activities are disclosed in note 1). The question arises whether such items might be displayed separately in the statement of income. This may be possible in some circumstances, by using a "boxed presentation" format, but this presentation should be used with caution.

5 Share capital

	Number of shares (000s)	$
Opening balance at January 1, 2010	257,131	250
Issued in financing	–	–
Issued on exercise of employee stock options	–	–
Balance at March 31, 2010	257,131	250
Opening balance at January 1, 2011	257,131	250
Issued in financing	3,846	50
Issued on exercise of employee stock options	455	5
Balance at March 31, 2011	261,432	305

On March 15, 2011, Sample Co. completed a private placement of equity, issuing a total of 3,846,154 shares for proceeds of $50 (net of share issue costs of $3).

(All amounts in millions of Canadian dollars)

6 Compensation of key management

Key management include the company's directors, members of the Executive Committee and the Head of Internal Audit. Compensation awarded to key management included:

	For the period ended March 31, 2011	For the period ended March 31, 2010
	$	$
Salaries and short-term employee benefits	14	12
Post-employment benefits	1	1
Share-based payments	4	2
Termination benefits	5	–
	24	15

PwC observation. In accordance with IAS 34.16 and 17(j), this disclosure would be required in interim financial statements when transactions with key management are material to an understanding of the current interim period or are unusual because of their nature, size or incidence. Compensation paid to key management represents related party transactions under IFRS, which should be taken into account in materiality assessments.

7 Income tax

Income tax expense is recognized based on management's best estimate of the weighted average annual income tax rate expected for the full financial year. The estimated average annual rate used for the year ended December 31, 2010 and the three months ended March 31, 2011 was 33%.

8 Financial instruments

During the period, the company's available-for-sale debt securities ceased being quoted in an active market and the fair value of the securities was reduced to $36 from $54 at December 31, 2010. As the securities were impaired at December 31, 2010, this further decrease in fair value of $18 has been recorded in net income during the period.

The fair value of the debt securities is measured using a discounted cash flow approach that incorporates available market information. As the market is not active, the company must estimate certain inputs to the valuation model, including the timing and amount of expected future cash flows, liquidity discount and credit spread used to determine the applicable discount factor to apply to the expected cash flows. In estimating the credit spread, the company reviewed various comparable debt securities and determined that the reasonably possible range of spreads applicable to the debt securities was 19.7% to 24.3%. A credit spread of 21% was applied in measuring the securities' fair value at March 31, 2011. If the company had used alternative credit spreads within the range, the effects on fair value would be as follows:

Credit spread	Fair value	Increase (decrease) from reported
%	$	$
19.7	38	2
21.0	36	–
24.3	33	(3)

(All amounts in millions of Canadian dollars)

As a result of the change in the observability of market information, the debt securities were reclassified from Level 2 to Level 3 during the period.

PwC observation. Existing IAS 34 does not provide any specific guidance about significant events and transactions affecting financial instruments that would require disclosure in interim financial statements. However, in its August, 2009 Exposure Draft, *Improvements to IFRS*, the IASB has proposed amending IAS 34 to explicitly consider financial instruments. The proposed amendments include examples of circumstances that would require financial instruments disclosures, such as significant changes in business or economic conditions affecting the fair values of an entity's financial instruments and significant transfers of an entity's financial instruments between levels of the fair value hierarchy. In its November, 2009 Exposure Draft, *Fair Value Measurement*, the IASB has proposed requiring annual fair value disclosures related to financial instruments in interim financial statements.

(All amounts in millions of Canadian dollars)

9 Segment reporting

The company is only involved in the manufacturing and sale of widgets. Segment information is provided on the basis of geographic segments as the company manages its widget business through three geographic regions – Canada, the United States and Europe. The business segments presented reflect the management structure of the company and the way in which the company's management reviews business performance. The company evaluates the performance of its operating segments primarily based on operating profit, as defined below.

Segment revenue

	March 31, 2011			
	Canada $	USA $	Europe $	Total $
External revenue	124	187	22	333
Inter-segment revenue	17	(14)	(3)	–
Total segment revenue	141	173	19	333

	March 31, 2010			
	Canada $	USA $	Europe $	Total $
External revenue	101	157	20	278
Inter-segment revenue	14	(12)	(2)	-
Total segment revenue	115	145	18	278

Segment profit

	March 31, 2011			
	Canada $	USA $	Europe $	Total $
Gross profit	32	47	6	85
General and administration	(8)	(18)	(1)	(27)
Sales and marketing	(8)	(11)	–	(19)
Research and development	(6)	(3)	–	(9)
Other gains and losses (net)	5	8	–	13
Segment profit	15	23	5	43

(All amounts in millions of Canadian dollars)

	March 31, 2010			
	Canada $	USA $	Europe $	Total $
Gross profit	19	34	4	57
General and administration	(7)	(16)	(1)	(24)
Sales and marketing	(5)	(9)	–	(14)
Research and development	(3)	(1)	–	(4)
Other gains and losses (net)	5	7	–	12
Segment profit	9	15	3	27

Reconciliation of operating profit to income (loss) before income tax

	March 31, 2011			
	Canada $	USA $	Europe $	Total $
Segment profit	15	23	5	43
Net interest expense	(4)	(2)	–	(6)
Share of income of associates	6	–	–	6
Income before income tax	17	21	5	43

	March 31, 2010			
	Canada $	USA $	Europe $	Total $
Segment profit	9	15	3	27
Net interest expense	(9)	(3)	–	(12)
Share of income of associates	10	–	–	10
Income before income tax	10	12	3	25

Assets by geography

	March 31, 2011			
	Canada $	USA $	Europe $	Total $
Total assets	1,080	1,871	164	3,115

	March 31, 2010			
	Canada $	USA $	Europe $	Total $
Total assets	1,158	1,996	160	3,314

(All amounts in millions of Canadian dollars)

10 Seasonality

The company's financial results for any individual quarter are not necessarily indicative of results to be expected for the full year. Interim period revenues and earnings are typically sensitive to regional and local weather, market conditions, and in particular, to cyclical variations in construction spending. Typically, the first quarter is the weakest quarter as construction and infrastructure activity requiring widgets is constrained in the winter months. This is followed by a pickup in the second quarter as construction and other contracts begin to be put out for bid and companies begin to prepare for summer activity. The third quarter generally tends to be slower, however, fourth quarter activity generally strengthens as companies make year-end capital spending decisions.

PwC observation. For an entity whose business is highly seasonal, IAS 34.21 encourages (but does not require) the reporting of financial information for the twelve months ending on the interim reporting date, with comparatives. Applying this requirement in the year of initial adoption of IFRS could affect the selection of an entity's date of transition to IFRS.

11 Dividends

A dividend of $0.50 per share, declared in January 2010, was paid in February 2011 (2010: $nil per share).

12 Acquisition of non-controlling interest

On March 31, 2011, the company acquired an additional 20% of the common shares of a subsidiary, X Limited, raising its equity interest to 80%, for cash consideration of $80. The carrying value of the net assets represented by the additional interest acquired was $50, which resulted in a charge of $30 to retained earnings.

13 Subsequent events

Subsequent to March 31, 2011, the fair value of the company's available-for-sale debt securities increased and, on April 15, 2011, the company disposed of the investments for proceeds of $45, which resulted in a gain of $9.

Interim reporting disclosure checklist

This disclosure checklist outlines the minimum disclosures required by IAS 34, 'Interim financial reporting', and other IFRSs published by the IASB up to and including March 2010 insofar as they affect interim reports. It also outlines the requirements of the Disclosure and Transparency Rules (DTR).

When preparing interim reports, consideration should be given to whether disclosure of the minimum information required by IAS 34 and the DTR is sufficient for the purposes of communication with investors. Additional IFRS-compliant information should be included when the information is necessary to help explain the current interim period's performance. This checklist is intended for general reference purposes only; it is not a substitute for reading the standards and interpretations themselves, or for professional judgement as to the fairness of presentation. Further specific information may be required in order to ensure fair presentation under IFRS depending on the circumstances.

This disclosure checklist does not deal with the measurement requirements of IFRS; a thorough understanding of international standards and interpretations that are relevant to the reporting entity's circumstances will be necessary. This checklist is presented in a format designed to facilitate the collection and review of disclosures for each component of the interim report. All disclosures have been grouped by subject, where appropriate. The references in the left-hand margin of the checklist refer to the paragraphs of the standards or DTR in which the disclosure requirements appear. Additional notes and explanations in the checklist are shown in *italics*.

The boxes in the right-hand margin of each page are designed to assist in completing the checklist. In the left-hand box (headed 'Y-NA-NM') one of the following should be entered for each disclosure item:

- **Y ('Yes')** – the appropriate disclosure has been made;
- **NA** ('Not applicable') – the item does not apply to the reporting entity; or
- **NM** ('Not material') – the item is regarded as not material to the interim report of the reporting entity.

Materiality is defined in IAS 1 paragraph 7, and in paragraphs 29 and 30 of the IASB's 'Framework for the preparation and presentation of financial statements'. Omissions or misstatements of items are material if they could, individually or collectively, influence the economic decisions that users make on the basis of the financial statements. Materiality depends on the size and nature of the item. IAS 1 paragraph 31 states that a specific disclosure requirement in a standard or an interpretation need not be satisfied if the information is not material. IAS 34 paragraph 23 requires that materiality, for the purpose of preparing the interim financial report, is assessed in relation to the results of the interim period and not in relation to the annual results.

The right-hand box on each page (headed 'Ref') can be used to insert a reference to the relevant part of the financial statements (such as 'Note 7') for all items that have been marked 'Y' in the left-hand box.

Interim reporting disclosure checklist

The DTR contain a number of exemptions from preparing half-yearly reports:

DTR TP 2 ■ Issuers of debt securities *only* that were admitted to the official list *before* 1 January 2005 (this transitional provision has effect for ten years following 1 January 2005).

DTR 4.4.2 ■ Issuers of wholesale debt only (denomination per unit is at least 50,000 euros, or an equivalent amount).

DTR 4.4.4 ■ Issuers already existing on 31 December 2003 that exclusively issue debt securities unconditionally and irrevocably guaranteed by the issuer's Home Member State or by a regional or local authority of that state on a regulated market.

DTR 4.4.3 ■ Credit institutions whose shares are not admitted to trading and that have, in a continuous or repeated manner, only issued debt securities, provided that:

- the total nominal amount of all such debt securities remains below 100,000,000 euros; and
- the credit institution has not published a prospectus in accordance with the prospectus directive.

DTR 4.4.1 ■ Public sector issuers such as a state, regional or local authority of a state, a public international body of which at least one EEA State is a member, the ECB and EEA States' national central banks.

DTR 4.4.5 ■ Issuers of transferable securities convertible into shares.

DTR 4.4.7 ■ Issuers of depository receipts.

DTR 4.4.8 ■ Issuers whose registered office is in a non-EEA State whose relevant laws are considered equivalent by the FSA. The FSA maintains a published list of non-EEA states that it judges to have equivalent laws.

Issuers of preference shares are subject to the rules on half-yearly financial reports but are exempt from preparing interim management statements. [DTR 4.4.6].

		Y-NA-NM	Ref
General			
IAS 34 paras 6, 7, 9, 10	An entity should publish in its interim report either:		
	(a) a complete set of financial statements (described in IAS 1); or		
	(b) a set of condensed financial statements (described in IAS 34).		
	Notes: *(a) If a complete set of financial statements is published in the interim report, the form and content of those statements should conform to the requirements of IAS 1 for a complete set of financial statements. All disclosures required by IAS 34 as well as all those required by other standards should be included.* *(b) If a condensed set of financial information is published in the interim report, as a minimum, disclosures required by IAS 34 should be included. Disclosures required by other IFRSs are not required for condensed interim financial information, except where they are material to an understanding of the current interim period.* *(c) If a complete set of financial statements is published, GAAPChecker should be completed in place of this checklist.*		

		Y-NA-NM	Ref
	(d) *The DTR do not expect a complete set of financial statements, so it would be very unusual to find an entity wishing to do this.*		
IAS 34 para 14	If the most recent annual financial statements were consolidated financial statements, is the interim report also prepared on a consolidated basis?		
CA06 S435	Where the interim report contains comparative information in respect of the previous financial year, does the interim report contain the following statements:		
	■ That the interim report is not the group's statutory accounts?		
	■ Whether or not the statutory accounts for the preceding financial year have been filed with the Registrar?		
	■ Whether or not the auditors have reported on the statutory accounts for the preceding financial year?		
	■ Whether or not the audit report on the statutory accounts for the preceding financial year was qualified, contained an emphasis of matter paragraph or contained a statement under either s498(2) (inadequate books and records or accounts not agreeing with records and returns) or s498(3) (inadequate information or explanations received by the auditor) of the Companies Act 2006?		
	Note: *Where interim reports include information for a full year (such as the balance sheet for the preceding financial year required by the DTR) that information falls within the definition of non-statutory information contained in CA06 s434 and the provisions that relate to non-statutory accounts will apply to that information.*		
Interim management report			
DTR 4.2.7	Does the interim management report include at least:		
	■ An indication of important events that have occurred during the first six months of the financial year, and their impact on the condensed set of financial statements?		
	■ A description of the principal risks and uncertainties for the remaining six months of the financial year?		
List! 18	Where the principal risks and uncertainties reported in the annual report remain valid at the interim reporting date, does the interim management report:		
	■ State that the principal risks and uncertainties have not changed?		
	■ Provide a summary of those principal risks and uncertainties?		
	■ Include a cross-reference to where a detailed explanation of the principal risks and uncertainties can be found in the annual report?		
DTR 4.2.8	For an issuer of shares, does the interim management report include the following information, as a minimum:		
	■ Related parties transactions that have taken place in the first six months of the current financial year and that have materially affected the financial position or the performance of the enterprise during that period?		
	■ Any changes in the related parties transactions described in the last annual report that could have a material effect on the financial position or performance of the enterprise in the first six months of the current financial year?		

		Y-NA-NM	Ref
	Note: *In relation to transactions described in the preceding paragraph information about such transactions may be aggregated according to their nature except where separate information is necessary for an understanding of the effects of related party transactions on the financial position of the entity.*		
Statement of comprehensive income			
IAS 34 paras 8, 20	Does the interim report include a condensed statement of comprehensive income prepared for the interim period and cumulatively for the current financial year to date presented as either:		
	(a) a condensed single statement; or		
	(b) a condensed separate income statement and a condensed statement of comprehensive income?		
	Notes: *(a) The same format should be followed in the interim statement of comprehensive income as was followed in the most recent annual financial statements (that is either as a single statement or a separate income statement and a statement of comprehensive income).* *(b) Where a condensed income statement is presented, this should be immediately before the statement of comprehensive income.*		
IAS 34 para 10	Does the condensed statement of comprehensive income include, at a minimum, each of the headings and subtotals that were included in the most recent annual financial statements?		
IAS 34 para 10	Does the condensed statement of comprehensive income include additional line items, without which the interim report would be misleading?		
IAS 34 para 20	Does the condensed statement of comprehensive income contain comparative information for the comparable interim periods (current period and financial year to date, if different) of the immediately preceding year?		
IAS 34 para 11	If IAS 33 is applicable, are basic and diluted earnings per share presented in the condensed statement of comprehensive income?		
IAS 34 para 11A	*Note:* *If an entity presents the components of profit or loss in a separate income statement it should present basic and diluted earnings per share in that separate statement.*		
Balance sheet			
IAS 34 paras 8, 20	Does the interim report include a condensed balance sheet prepared as at the end of the interim period?		
IAS 34 para 10	Does the condensed balance sheet include, at a minimum, each of the headings and subtotals that were included in the most recent annual financial statements?		
IAS 34 para 10	Does the condensed balance sheet include additional line items, without which the interim report would be misleading?		
IAS 34 para 20	Does the condensed balance sheet contain comparative information as at the end of the immediately preceding financial year?		
Statement of changes in equity			
IAS 34 para 8	Does the interim report include a condensed statement of changes in equity showing all changes in equity?		

		Y-NA-NM	Ref
IAS 34 para 10	Does the condensed statement of changes in equity include, at a minimum, each of the headings and subtotals that were included in the most recent annual financial statements?		
IAS 34 para 10	Does the condensed statement of changes in equity include additional line items, without which the interim report would be misleading?		
IAS 34 para 20	Is the condensed statement of changes in equity prepared cumulatively for the financial year to date?		
IAS 34 para 20	Is a comparative statement of changes in equity for the comparable year-to-date period of the immediately preceding financial year included in the interim report?		
Statement of cash flows			
IAS 34 paras 8, 20	Does the interim report include a condensed statement of cash flows prepared cumulatively for the current financial year to date?		
IAS 34 para 10	Does the condensed statement of cash flows include, at a minimum, each of the headings and subtotals that were included in the most recent annual financial statements?		
IAS 34 para 10	Does the condensed statement of cash flows include additional line items, without which the interim report would be misleading?		
IAS 34 para 20	Does the condensed statement of cash flows show comparative information for the comparable year-to-date period of the immediately preceding financial year?		
Explanatory notes			
IAS 34 para 15	*IAS 34 assumes that a reader of the interim report will also have access to the most recent annual financial statements. It is not necessary for the notes to duplicate information already given in the most recent annual financial statements. Instead, an explanation of material events and transactions that are significant to an understanding of the changes in financial position and performance since the last annual financial statements should be given.*		
IAS 34 paras 6, 15	Does the interim report focus on new activities, events and circumstances and provide explanations of events and transactions that are significant to an understanding of the changes in financial position and performance of the entity since the last annual reporting date?		
IAS 34 paras 6, 15 List! 18	Does the interim report include a discussion of the effect of economic turbulence and market conditions, liquidity difficulties or any going concern issues, together with management's plans for addressing them?		
IAS 34 paras 8, 19	Does the interim report contain a basis of preparation paragraph that states clearly whether the interim report has been prepared in accordance with IAS 34?		
IAS 34 para 19	*Note:* *An interim report should not be described as complying with IFRS unless it complies with all the requirements of each applicable standard and each applicable IFRIC interpretation.*		
IAS 34 para 16(a); DTR 4.2.6	Does the interim report contain a statement that the same accounting policies, methods of computation and presentation have been followed in its preparation as were applied in the most recent annual financial statements; or, if those policies, methods or presentation have been changed, include a description of the nature and effect of the change?		

		Y-NA-NM	Ref
IAS 34 para 43	*Notes:* *(a) A change in accounting policy, other than one for which the transition is specified by a new Standard or Interpretation should be effected by restating the comparative information presented in the interim report in accordance with IAS 8.* *(b) DTR 4.2.6 allows consistency not to be applied where (1) the accounting policies and presentation are to be changed in the subsequent annual financial statements, in which case the new accounting policies and presentation should be followed and the changes and the reasons for the changes should be disclosed in the half-yearly report, or (2) the FSA otherwise agrees.*		
IAS 34 para 16(b)	Does the interim report contain explanatory comments about the seasonality or cyclicality of interim operations?		
IAS 34 para 21	*Note:* *Financial information for the 12 months ending on the interim reporting date and comparative information for the prior 12-month period may be useful for an entity whose business is highly seasonal. Such entities are encouraged to consider reporting such information in addition to the information required by IAS 34 para 20.*		
IAS 34 para 16(c)	Does the interim report contain the nature and amount of items occurring in the financial year-to-date affecting assets, liabilities, equity, net income, or cash flows that are unusual because of their nature, size, or incidence?		
IAS 34 para 17(d)	Does the interim report contain details of any property, plant and equipment acquired or disposed of during the financial year to date?		
IAS 34 para 17(e)	Does the interim report contain details of any commitments to purchase property, plant and equipment after the end of the interim period?		
IAS 34 para 16(d)	Does the interim report contain the nature and amount of changes in estimates of amounts reported in prior interim periods of the current year, or in prior years, if those changes have a material effect in the current interim period (for example, changes in estimates relating to inventory write-downs, impairment losses, provision re-estimates etc)?		
IAS 34 paras 16(j), 17(f)	Does the interim report contain details of changes in contingent liabilities and contingent assets, including litigation settlements, since the last annual balance sheet date?		
IAS 34 para 17(i)	Does the interim report contain details of any loan default or breach of a loan agreement since the last annual balance sheet date that has not been remedied on or before the end of the interim period?		
IAS 34 para 16(e)	Does the interim report contain details of issuances, repurchases, and repayments of debt and equity securities since the last annual balance sheet date?		
IAS 34 para 16(f)	Does the interim report contain details of dividends paid (aggregate or per share), separately for ordinary shares and other shares during the financial year to date?		
IAS 34 para 16(h)	Does the interim report contain details of material events subsequent to the end of the interim period that have not been reflected in the interim financial statements?		
IAS 34 para 16(i)	Does the interim report detail the effect of changes in the composition of the entity during the interim period (for example, business combinations, acquisitions and disposals of subsidiaries and long-term investments, restructurings and discontinued operations)?		

		Y-NA-NM	Ref
IAS 34 para 17(g)	Does the interim report contain details of the correction of prior period errors (as defined in IAS 8)?		
IAS 34 para 17(j)	Does the interim report contain details of related party transactions (as defined in IAS 24) for the financial year-to-date?		
IAS 34 para 16	Does the interim report contain details of any other events or transactions that are material to an understanding of the current interim period?		
Segment information			
	Does the interim report contain:		
IAS 34 para 16(g)(i)	■ Revenues from external customers, if included in the measure of segment profit or loss provided to the chief operating decision maker?		
IAS 34 para 16(g)(ii)	■ Intersegment revenues, if included in the measure of segment profit or loss provided to the chief operating decision maker?		
IAS 34 para 16(g)(iii)	■ A measure of segment profit or loss?		
IAS 34 para 16(g)(iv)	■ Total assets for which there has been a material change from the amount disclosed in the last annual financial statements?		
IAS 34 para 16(g)(v)	■ A description of the differences from the last annual financial statements in the basis of segmentation or in the basis of measurement of segment profit or loss?		
IAS 34 para 16(g)(vi)	■ A reconciliation of the total of the reportable segments' profit or loss to the entity's profit or loss before tax and discontinued operations, with material reconciling items separately identified and described?		
IFRS 8 para 29 IFRS 8 para 30	*Notes:* (a) *If an entity changes the structure of its internal organisation such that the composition of its reportable segments change, the corresponding information for earlier periods, including interim periods, should be restated unless the information is not available and the cost to develop it would be excessive.* (b) *Following a change in reportable segments, an entity should disclose whether it has restated the corresponding amounts. If corresponding amounts are not restated, the entity shall disclose current period segment information on both the old and new bases, unless the information is not available and the cost to develop it would be excessive.*		
IFRS 3 (revised)			
	For each business combination that was effected during the period (or after the reporting period but before the financial statements are authorised for issue) does the entity disclose:		
IFRS 3 para B64(a)	■ The name and a description of the acquiree?		
IFRS3 para B64(b)	■ The acquisition date?		
IFRS3 para B64(c)	■ The percentage of voting equity interests acquired?		
IFRS3 para B64(d)	■ The primary reasons for the business combination and a description of how the acquirer obtained control of the acquiree?		

		Y-NA-NM	Ref
IFRS 3 para B64(e)	■ A qualitative description of the factors that make up the goodwill recognised, such as expected synergies from combining operations of the acquiree and the acquirer, and intangible assets that do not qualify for separate recognition or other factor?		
IFRS 3 para B64(f)	For each business combination that was effected during the period (or after the reporting period but before the financial statements are authorised for issue) does the entity disclose the acquisition-date fair value of the total consideration transferred and the acquisition-date fair value of each major class of consideration?		
	This includes items such as:		
	(a) Cash;		
	(b) Other tangible or intangible assets, including a business or subsidiary of the acquirer;		
	(c) Liabilities incurred – for example, a liability for contingent consideration; and		
	(d) Equity interests of the acquirer, including the number of instruments or interests issued or issuable and the method of determining the fair value of those instruments or interests.		
	For each business combination that was effected during the period (or after the reporting period but before the financial statements are authorised for issue), for contingent consideration arrangements and indemnification assets, does the entity disclose:		
IFRS 3para B64(g)	■ The amount recognised as of the acquisition date?		
IFRS 3 para B64(g)	■ A description of the arrangement and the basis for determining the amount of the payment?		
IFRS 3 para B64	■ An estimate of the range of outcomes (undiscounted) or, if a range cannot be estimated, that fact and the reasons why a range cannot be estimated? If the maximum amount of the payment is unlimited, the acquirer discloses that fact.		
	For each business combination that was effected during the period (or after the reporting period but before the financial statements are authorised for issue), for acquired receivables does the entity disclose:		
	Note: *The disclosures should be provided by major class of receivable, such as loans, direct finance leases and any other class of receivables.*		
IFRS 3 para B64(h)	■ The fair value of the receivables?		
IFRS 3 para B64 (h)	■ The gross contractual amounts receivable?		
IFRS 3 para B64(h)	■ The best estimate at the acquisition date of the contractual cash flows not expected to be collected?		
IFRS 3 para B64(i)	For each business combination that was effected during the period (or after the reporting period but before the financial statements are authorised for issue) does the entity disclose the amounts recognised as of the acquisition date for each major class of assets acquired and liabilities assumed?		
	For each business combination that was effected during the period (or after the reporting period but before the financial statements are authorised for issue), and for each contingent liability recognised in accordance with IFRS 3 do the financial statements include:		

		Y-NA-NM	Ref
IFRS 3 para B64(j)	■ A brief description of the nature of the obligation and of the expected timing of any resulting outflows of economic benefits?		
	Note: *This would normally be expected to include disclosure of likely settlement period and discount rate (if used).*		
IFRS 3 para B64(j)	■ An indication of the uncertainties about the amount or timing of those outflows (where necessary to provide adequate information, disclose the major assumptions made concerning future events)?		
IFRS 3 para B64(j)	■ The amount of any expected reimbursement, stating the amount of any asset that has been recognised for that expected reimbursement?		
IFRS 3 para B64(j)	■ Except where the possibility of any outflow in settlement is remote, the following information about each class of contingent liability:		
	(a) A brief description of the nature of the contingent liability;		
	(b) Where practicable		
	(i) an estimate of its financial effect, measured under IAS 37 paragraphs 36-52,		
	(ii) an indication of the uncertainties about the amount or timing of any outflow, and		
	(iii) the possibility of any reimbursement; and		
	(c) Where relevant, the fact that the information is not disclosed because it is not practicable to do so?		
IFRS 3 para 64(k)	For each business combination that was effected during the period (or after the reporting period but before the financial statements are authorised for issue), does the entity disclose the total amount of goodwill that is expected to be deductible for tax purposes?		
	For each business combination that was effected during the period, for transactions that are recognised separately from the acquisition of assets and assumption of liabilities in the business combination in accordance with IFRS 3 para 51, does the entity disclose:		
IFRS 3 para B64(l)	■ A description of each transaction?		
IFRS 3 para B64(l)	■ How the acquirer accounted for each transaction?		
IFRS 3 para B64(l)	■ The amounts recognised for each transaction and the line item in the financial statements in which each amount is recognised?		
IFRS 3 para B64(l)	■ If the transaction is the effective settlement of a pre-existing relationship, the method used to determine the settlement amount?		
IFRS 3 para B64(m)	The disclosure of separately recognised transactions includes the amount of acquisition-related costs and, separately, the amount of those costs recognised as an expense and the line item or items in the statement of comprehensive income in which those expenses are recognised. Are the amount of any issue costs not recognised as an expense and how they were recognised disclosed?		

		Y-NA-NM	Ref
	For each business combination that was effected during the period (or after the reporting period but before the financial statements are authorised for issue), and which resulted in a bargain purchase, does the entity disclose:		
IFRS 3 para B64(n)	■ The amount of any gain recognised in accordance with IFRS 3 para 34 and the line item in the statement of comprehensive income in which the gain is recognised?		
IFRS 3 para B64(n)	■ A description of the reasons why the transaction resulted in a gain?		
	For each business combination that was effected during the period (or after the reporting period but before the financial statements are authorised for issue), for each business combination in which the acquirer holds less than 100% of the equity interest in the acquiree at the acquisition date, does the entity disclose:		
	Note: *A non-controlling interest is defined as the equity in a subsidiary not attributable, directly or indirectly to a parent.*		
IFRS 3 para B64(o)	■ The amount of the non-controlling interest in the acquiree recognised at the acquisition date and the measurement basis for that amount?		
IFRS 3 para B64(o)	■ For each non-controlling interest in an acquiree measured at fair value, the valuation techniques and key model inputs used for determining that value?		
	For each business combination that was effected during the period (or after the reporting period but before the financial statements are authorised for issue), does the entity disclose:		
IFRS 3 para B64(p)	■ The acquisition-date fair value of the equity interest in the acquiree held by the acquirer immediately before the acquisition date?		
IFRS 3 para B64(p)	■ The amount of any gain or loss recognised as a result of remeasuring to fair value the equity interest in the acquiree held by the acquirer before the business combination and the line item in the statement of comprehensive income in which that gain or loss is recognised?		
	For each business combination that was effected during the period (or after the reporting period but before the financial statements are authorised for issue), does the entity disclose:		
IFRS 3 para B64(q)	■ The amounts of revenue and profit or loss of the acquiree since the acquisition date included in the consolidated statement of comprehensive income for the reporting period?		
IFRS 3 para B64(q)	■ The revenue and profit or loss of the combined entity for the current reporting period as though the acquisition date for all business combinations that occurred during the year had been as of the beginning of the annual reporting period?		
	Note: *If obtaining any of the information required is impracticable, the acquirer discloses that fact and explains why the disclosure is impracticable.*		
IFRS 3 para B66	If the acquisition date of a business combination is after the end of the reporting period but before the financial statements are authorised for issue, has the acquirer disclosed:		
	■ Whether the initial accounting for the business combination is incomplete at the time the financial statements are authorised for issue?		

		Y-NA-NM	Ref
	■ Which disclosures could not be made and the reasons why they cannot be made?		
	For adjustments recognised in the current reporting period or previous reporting periods in relation to a business combination, does the acquirer disclose the following for each material business combination or in aggregate for individually immaterial business combinations that are material collectively:		
IFRS 3 para B67(a)	■ If the initial accounting for a business combination is incomplete for particular assets, liabilities, non-controlling interests or items of consideration and the amounts recognised in the financial statements for the business combination have been determined only provisionally:		
	(a) The reasons why the initial accounting for the business combination is incomplete;		
	(b) The assets, liabilities, equity interests or items of consideration for which the initial accounting is incomplete; and		
	(c) The nature and amount of any measurement period adjustments recognised during the reporting period?		
IFRS 3 para B67(b)	■ For each reporting period after the acquisition date until the entity collects, sells or otherwise loses the right to a contingent consideration asset, or until the entity settles a contingent consideration liability or the liability is cancelled or expires:		
	(a) Any changes in the recognised amounts, including any differences arising upon settlement;		
	(b) Any changes in the range of outcomes (undiscounted) and the reasons for those changes; and		
	(c) The valuation techniques and key model inputs used to measure contingent consideration?		
	Does the acquirer disclose for contingent liabilities recognised in a business combination, the following information for each class of provision:		
IFRS 3 para B67(c)	■ For each class of provision, an entity discloses:		
	(a) The carrying amount at the beginning and end of the period;		
	(b) Additional provisions made in the period, including increases to existing provisions;		
	(c) Amounts used (that is, incurred and charged against the provision) during the period;		
	(d) Unused amounts reversed during the period; and		
	(e) The increase during the period in the discounted amount arising from the passage of time and the effect of any change in the discount rate.		
IFRS 3 para B64(j)	■ A brief description of the nature of the obligation and of the expected timing of any resulting outflows of economic benefits?		
	Note: *This is normally expected to include disclosure of likely settlement period and discount rate (if used).*		
IFRS 3 para B64(j)	■ An indication of the uncertainties about the amount or timing of those outflows (where necessary to provide adequate information, disclose the major assumptions made concerning future events)?		

		Y-NA-NM	Ref
	■ The amount of any expected reimbursement, stating the amount of any asset that has been recognised for that expected reimbursement?		
	For adjustments recognised in the current reporting period or previous reporting periods in relation to a business combination, and for each material business combination or in aggregate for individually immaterial business combinations that are material collectively, does the acquirer disclose a reconciliation of the carrying amount of goodwill at the beginning and end of the reporting period showing separately:		
IFRS 3 para B67(d)	■ The gross amount and accumulated impairment losses at the beginning of the reporting period?		
IFRS 3 para B67(d)	■ Additional goodwill recognised during the reporting period, except goodwill included in a disposal group that, on acquisition, meets the criteria to be classified as held for sale in accordance with IFRS 5?		
IFRS 3 para B67(d)	■ Adjustments resulting from the subsequent recognition of deferred tax assets during the reporting period in accordance with IFRS 3 para 67?		
IFRS 3 para B67(d)	■ Goodwill included in a disposal group classified as held for sale in accordance with IFRS 5 and goodwill derecognised during the reporting period without having previously been included in a disposal group classified as held for sale?		
IFRS 3 para B67(d)	■ Impairment losses recognised during the reporting period in accordance with IAS 36?		
IFRS 3 para B67(d)	■ If any portion of the goodwill recognised in a business combination during the period has not been allocated to a cash-generating unit (group of units) at the reporting date, does the acquirer disclose the amount of the unallocated goodwill together with the reasons why that amount remains unallocated?		
IFRS 3 para B67(d)	■ Net exchange rate differences arising during the reporting period in accordance with IAS 21?		
IFRS 3 para B67(d)	■ Any other changes in the carrying amount during the reporting period?		
IFRS 3 para B67(d)	■ The gross amount and accumulated impairment losses at the end of the reporting period?		
IFRS 3 para B67(e)	For adjustments recognised in the current reporting period or previous reporting periods in relation to a business combination, and for each material business combination or in the aggregate for individually immaterial business combinations that are material collectively, does the acquirer disclose the amount and an explanation of any gain or loss recognised in the current reporting period that both:		
	(a) Relates to the identifiable assets acquired or liabilities assumed in a business combination that was effected in the current or previous reporting period; and		
	(b) Is of such a size, nature or incidence that disclosure is relevant to understanding the combined entity's financial statements?		
IFRS 3 para B63	If the specific disclosures required by this and other IFRSs do not enable users of the financial statements to evaluate the nature and financial effect of business combinations and of the impact of any adjustments arising from them, does the acquirer disclose whatever additional information is necessary to meet those objectives?		